MW01017553

H. Jose 6/90

HOMEMAKING RESEARCH LABORATORIES
TONY, WI 54563 CALL 800-255-9929
KITCHEN TOOLS IDEAS
CATALOG NO. 109-0063

kitchen tools

kitchen tools

cooking with a twist and a flair!

Patricia Gentry

Photographs by Craig Mohr
Illustrations by Pamela Manley

101 Productions

Frontispiece I: Salmon Fillets with Tangerine and Ginger
Beurre Blanc; green onion fans
Frontispiece II: Melon Soup with Strawberries

Copyright © 1988 Chevron Chemical Company
Cover design: Gary Hespenheide
Cover photography: Chuck Undersee
Text design: Lynne O'Neil

Inside photographs courtesy of Damco Manufacturing
Food styling: Patricia Gentry and Marilyn Smith
Fruits and vegetables: Tanaka Quality Produce, Santa Monica, Calif.
Flowers: Flowers on Ashford, Santa Monica, Calif.

All rights reserved under international and Pan-American copyright
conventions.
No part of this book may be reproduced in any form without the written
permission of 101 Productions.
Printed and bound in the U.S.A.
Published by 101 Productions and distributed by Ortho Information
Services, Box 5047, San Ramon, CA 94583

Library of Congress Catalog Card Number 88-71973
ISBN 0-89721-171-5

To The Cheering Section: Larry, Tracy, Mark, Chelcea and Kirsten

ACKNOWLEDGMENTS

Larry, Tracy and Mark: my family, the willing guinea pigs.

Marilyn Smith: proofreading, food styling and friendship.

Elizabeth, Helen, Lorraine, Robin, Polly, Yvonne, Florence, Marilin, Mary, Betsy, Ruth and Frances: students and friends with words of encouragement.

Grace and Linda: my department chairmen, for room to grow and experiment.

Carol and Barbara: coworkers with words of encouragement.

Carolyn and Bill: instructors in gourmet food and wine classes and enthusiastic supporters.

Vic and Marylou: my encouraging parents who allowed me to experiment and create in the home kitchen.

Bernd and Debbie Dressler, Irene, Loni and Mark: Damco Manufacturing– Dressler Marketing.

Jane Horn: editing.

contents

introduction

This book is about creative, artistic and fun food preparation and presentation, and the use of all those kitchen tools that may have been pushed to the back of the kitchen drawer or are still hanging on the rack at the store because the cook didn't know what to do with them. There are literally hundreds of tools and gadgets for sale in cookware shops and housewares departments. Even experienced cooks are often overwhelmed by the sheer number of what's available to them. What *is* this tool? What specific tasks does this tool perform? Do I need this tool?

From my cooking classes and from conversations with other food professionals, it became clear that a guide to kitchen tools—how to identify them, how to use them— would be enormously helpful. This illustrated, ready reference is offered as that guide.

Included are familiar kitchen generalists like spatulas and whisks that are basic to food preparation and used constantly. Also described are those little gems, like food ballers and peelers, that once used and understood become indispensable. You will also learn about those tools that excel at one specific task. These are needed less frequently, but often hold a special place in the cook's heart because they do their job so well (just ask a baker who loves cherry pie if anything could replace a cherry pitter). Many tools are very versatile and you may learn new ways to use old stand-bys.

I am picturing that the kitchens of those who will use this book are equipped with food processors and/ or blenders and electric mixers, and I have written recipe directions that refer to the use of these machines. These appliances are wonderful for quantity preparation, and save endless hours of time-consuming mixing, beating and chopping. Sometimes, however, a small job is more efficiently or precisely done with a hand tool. This is the cook's decision.

I have classified a few items as tools—things like wooden spoons, rubber scrapers, rolling pins—because I feel they are essential for specific techniques. Very basic equipment, such as measuring cups and spoons, are not included as most cooks know how to use them. Cookware, baking sheets and pans and serving tools are not listed because they are outside of the book's focus.

This is also intended as a versatile cookbook that will provide hands-on experience with many of the tools and techniques covered in the book's first two sections. The recipes that appear here are a blend of family favorites and those developed over the ten years I have spent teaching gourmet cooking in the Los Angeles area. From my students I've acquired a wealth of material about ethnic and regional cooking, particularly the foods of Latin America, Asia and the Middle East. I've also been inspired by travels throughout the wine-producing areas of California and by conversations with winemakers, restaurateurs and our state's creative young chefs, undertaken as background for my classes in "California Cuisine."

As you read and research the recipes, always remember that the freshest of ingredients will assure optimum flavors, and that kitchen tools will turn kitchen work into a creative, artistic and enjoyable experience. Create and enjoy!

THE HAND TOOLS INCLUDED in this selective listing have proven their value in the kitchen. You won't find a description of every tool that is manufactured—only those that have been tested by time and have endured because there are no better replacements.

Browse these entries as you would a catalog. It's an opportunity to identify tools you've seen or heard of, but never worked with, and to learn new ways to use those that are more familiar to you. It's not expected that every kitchen will be equipped with every tool, nor is this necessary. Which tools to buy? The ones that accomplish the culinary chores you do most often faster, easier and more efficiently.

tools

Apple Slicer and Corer

Bowl Chopper

Pastry Brush

Bulb Baster

APPLE SLICER AND CORER

• Slices and cores apples in one action.

BIRD'S NEST MAKER

This tool consists of two nested wire strainers. Material to be nested is placed between the two wire strainers and deep fried.

• Forms potato, noodle and bread baskets to hold entrées, vegetables and salads.

BOWL CHOPPER

Used in conjunction with a small wooden bowl. The same tasks may be done with a chef's knife or for large quantities, a food processor.

• Chops fresh herbs, garlic and shallots, nuts.

BRUSHES

MUSHROOM
• Used to brush grit off of mushrooms.

PASTRY
Buy top quality, flat, natural-bristle brushes. Inexpensive plastic brushes will tear fragile pastry. Feather pastry brushes are available for very delicate work.

• Used to brush marinades on meats, fish, poultry and vegetables.
• Used to brush melted butter on fine pastry, bread, cookie and filo dough.
• Used to brush warm glazes on fruit tarts and other pastries.

BULB BASTER
WITH INJECTING NEEDLE

• Bastes poultry and roasts with pan juices.
• Skims fat from soups and stews.
• Injects marinade or liquid seasoning into poultry and roasts.
• Injects fruits, especially melons, with fruit juices or spirits.

COLANDERS, CHINA CAP, CHINOIS, SIEVES, STRAINERS

COLANDERS
• A colander is a metal or plastic bowl with large holes and is used to drain cooked vegetables, fruits and pastas.
• Holds vegetables to be quick-blanched (rinsed with boiling water).
• Holds foods to be cleaned and rinsed.

Colander

Chinois

China Cap

Tea Strainer

Sieve

CHINA CAP
(cone-shaped sieve)
• Used to strain liquids. The cone shape helps force the liquid down through the strainer.

CHINOIS
(cone-shaped sieve made of fine mesh)
• Used with a pestle for pureeing fruits, vegetables and soups. This tool has been somewhat replaced by the blender and food processor; however, for maximum smoothness in soups and sauces this is the tool that will do the job.

SIEVES AND STRAINERS
Sieves are available in a large, round drum shape or smaller bowl shape. They differ from colanders in that they are made of wire mesh and have finer openings. Some have handles.
• Strains cooked foods.
• Sieves hardcooked egg yolk for garnish.
• Separates fine particles from larger particles.
• Used to sift or sprinkle confectioners' sugar and flour.

TEA STRAINER
• Strains small amounts of liquid.
• Sieves small amounts of egg yolk.

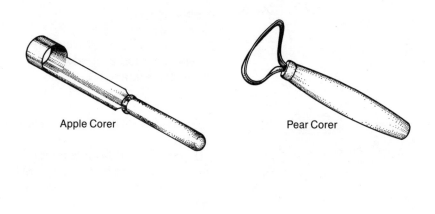

Apple Corer

Pear Corer

Tomato Corer

Zucchini Corer

Corn Kernel Remover

Crinkle Chip Cutter

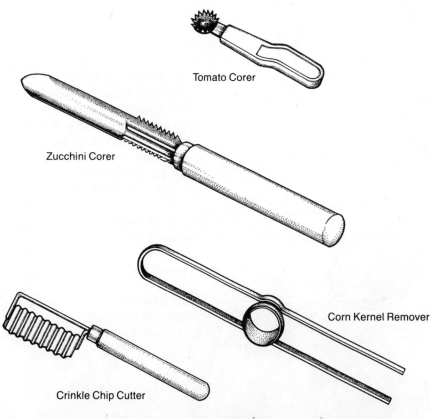

CORERS

APPLE
• Removes cores from apples and pears. Most apple corers cut approximately 3¼ inches in depth, and therefore cannot be used for long vegetables like cucumbers and zucchini.
• Removes plugs from melons to be filled with fruit juices or spirits.

PEAR
• Removes cores from pears. Cutting edge is shaped like the core of a pear.

TOMATO
• Removes seeds from tomatoes, particularly cherry tomatoes intended for stuffing.
• Can be used as a scraping tool to hollow-out vegetables.

ZUCCHINI
• Removes seeds from cucumbers and zucchini. The long cutting shaft of this tool removes the centers from cucumbers and zucchini, creating a hollow which can then be stuffed with meat or cheese fillings.

CORN KERNEL REMOVER

• Cuts and scrapes corn kernels from the cob.

CRINKLE CHIP CUTTER

• Prepares decorative slices and sticks of fruits and vegetables.
• Cuts fresh cucumber slices for pickles.
• Cuts decorative slices of some soft cheeses.
• Used as a garnishing tool.

CUTTERS

ASPIC-TRUFFLE
• Cuts jellied aspic and truffles into decorative shapes.
• Cuts pastry into decorative shapes.
• Cuts fruit and vegetable garnishes.

BISCUIT AND COOKIE
Cuts biscuit, cookie, yeast and pastry dough.
• Cuts fruit and vegetable garnishes.

CITRUS SHELL
• Separates citrus fruit from skin, creating two half shells for use as containers.

FRENCH BEAN
• Cuts beans in lengthwise strips and removes the strings.

Egg Separators

EGG SEPARATOR

• Separates egg white from yolk. The egg white drops through the open slots into a cup or bowl.
• Some egg separators are a combination tool with a pointed handle that can be used to lightly beat eggs.

FOOD MILL, FOOD GRINDER, MINCERS, ROTARY GRATER

FOOD MILL
This tool has been largely replaced by the blender and food processor.
• Purees soups, cooked vegetables and fruits.
• Grinds fruits for jam.

FOOD GRINDER
This tool has been largely replaced by the food processor.
• Grinds meats, vegetables and fruits.
• Makes bread, cookie and cake crumbs.

MINCERS
There are a variety of mincers available, but some can be difficult to clean. It's often quicker to use a chef's knife for small quantities and a food processor for large quantities.
• Chops and minces fresh herbs and parsley.

ROTARY GRATER
• Grates small amounts of hard cheese.
• Grinds nuts.
• Grates chocolate.

GARLIC PRESS

• Produces the finest pieces of minced garlic. In recipes the term is *pressed* garlic.
• Extracts juice and essence from fresh ginger.
• Some garlic presses are self cleaning.

Garlic Press

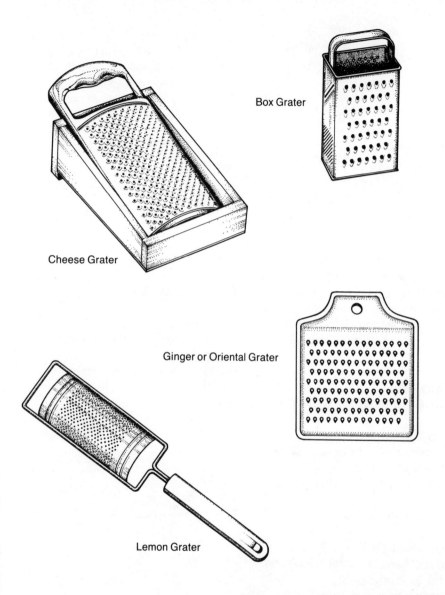

Box Grater

Cheese Grater

Ginger or Oriental Grater

Lemon Grater

GRATER-SHREDDERS

Graters come flat or curved with one size grating hole, or four-sided (box) with the holes on each side sized for particular tasks. Some graters are set in a wooden frame with a drawer that catches the grated food.

• *Small grating holes*: grated citrus zest and spices.
• *Medium grating holes*: larger pieces of citrus zest, hard cheeses, grated onion and chocolate.
• *Large grating holes*: grated fruits and vegetables for salads and nut breads, grated cheese.
• *Slicing slot*: sliced firm vegetables, shredded lettuce and cabbage.

GINGER OR ORIENTAL GRATER
• Grates ginger and extracts ginger juice. This grater has very sharp teeth and a small indentation at the bottom to catch ginger juice as the ginger is grated.

LEMON GRATER
• Grates lemon and other citrus zest, hard cheeses. This grater is attached to a long handle, which makes it easy to hold while grating small amounts of zest or cheese.

NUTMEG GRATER

• Grates nutmeg. Some nutmeg graters have a separate compartment at the top for holding the whole nutmeg.

HAMMER-POUNDER-TENDERIZER

• Flat side is used to pound boneless meat to a desired thickness.
• Pronged side is used to break up tough meat fibers in less tender cuts of meat.
• A disk-shaped pounder is also available.

KITCHEN SCISSORS
POULTRY SHEARS

KITCHEN SCISSORS
• Cuts up or quarters poultry.
• Cuts bread, cookie and pastry dough.
• Cuts leaves for garnishes.
• Used to snip parsley, chives and other herbs.

POULTRY SHEARS
• Cuts up or quarters poultry.

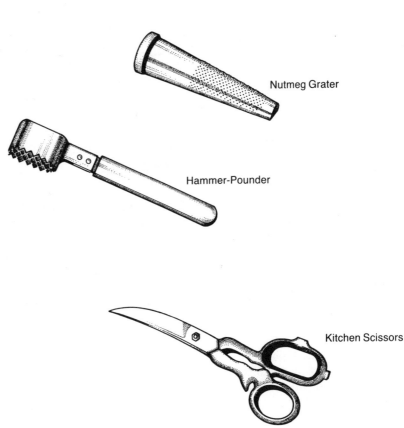

Nutmeg Grater

Hammer-Pounder

Kitchen Scissors

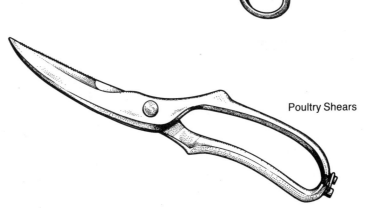

Poultry Shears

KNIVES

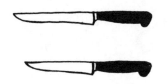

BONING
The boning knife has a narrower blade than other knives of the same size.
• Bones meats and poultry.

BREAD
• Neatly slices bread and rolls, filo dough, tomatoes and cucumbers.
• Excellent for slicing genoise and other cakes into thin layers.

CARVING
• Carves roasts, fish, thick steaks and poultry.
• Cuts and slices large fruits and vegetables.

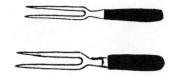

CARVING FORK
• Used with the carving knife. Holds meat steady.

CHEF'S
Comes in 6-inch, 8-inch and 10-inch lengths. Try each size for comfort and balance in the hand. The 8-inch knife is the most popular, but the 6-inch knife is very versatile.
• Chops, dices and minces.
• Pares and slices (6 inch).

CHESTNUT
• Used to pierce and peel chestnuts.

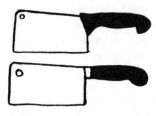

CLEAVERS
(standard)
These are heavy-duty cleavers. They should be sharpened like an ax, not a knife.
• Used for heavy chopping, particularly through bones.
• Used to chop frozen foods.

CLEAVER
(Oriental Vegetable Knife or *Usuba*)
These are lightweight knives or cleavers with a sharpened edge. They are not meant to cut or chop through bones. Oriental cooks do almost all of their food preparation with these knives.
• Chops, dices, minces and slices.
• Use (with practice) for preparing garnishes.
• Use the side of the knife for pounding and mashing.

FILLETING
This knife has a very flexible blade and must be sharp to work well. Because it is flexible, it easily makes angled cuts.
• Fillets meat and fish.
• Used as a garnishing tool.

FRUIT
Most fruit knives have a serrated edge.
• Cuts thin slices of apple, pear and other fruits.
• Sections citrus fruits.
• Slices tomatoes.

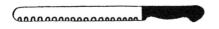

GRANTON-EDGE SLICER
This knife has a patented hollow ground edge with 1-inch flutes running vertically up the blade. The flutes allow the blade to glide more freely.
• Used to slice roast beef, turkey, chicken and ham, where very thin slices are desired.

GRAPEFRUIT
• Sections citrus fruit halves.
• Used to hollow-out vegetables, such as red cabbage or head lettuce.
• Cuts and removes pineapple meat, leaving a shell to be used as a container.

OYSTER
• Opens oysters and clams.

PARING
• Cuts or pares small hand-held foods.
• Used as a mini-chopper
• Bones small food items such as chicken legs and chicken wings.

PARING: CURVED
• Used to prepare garnishes and carve vegetables and fruits.
• Cuts tomato peel in a continuous strip for tomato roses.

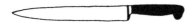

SLICING
This knife has a slightly flexible blade.
• Slices poultry and meats.
• Cuts large fruits and vegetables.

UTILITY
This knife is similar to the paring knife, only longer. It is sometimes called a sandwich knife.
• Cuts and slices fruits, vegetables, small breads and rolls.

SHARPENING STEEL
This is the most important tool for keeping knives sharp. A sharpening steel is not a grinding tool. It will realign a turned or bent edge on a knife that is dull. With a quality knife a few strokes on a steel will realign and sharpen the edge.

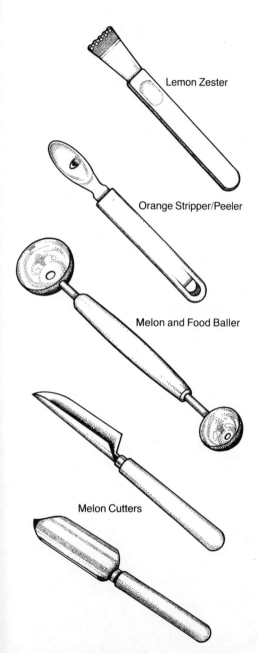

Lemon Zester

Orange Stripper/Peeler

Melon and Food Baller

Melon Cutters

LEMON ZESTER
ORANGE STRIPPER/PEELER

Different manufacturers have different names for these tools. Generally, the tools with a single opening that cuts a ¼-inch strip of citrus zest are stripper-peelers. The cutting tools with four or five small, round cutting edges that produce very fine pieces of citrus zest are zesters. Combination stripper-zesters are available as well.
• Cuts strips of peel or zest (the outer colored layer of the peel) from citrus fruits.
• Flutes mushrooms (stripper).
• Removes pits from stone fruits (peaches, nectarines).
• Used as a sculpturing tool for garnishing.

MANDOLINE

The mandoline has been around for a long time. It is a hand-operated slicing machine with one or more adjustable blades. Some have a corrugated blade to produce ruffled slices. The food processor with its choice of cutting disks has taken over many of the tasks of the mandoline.

• Slices firm fruits and vegetables.
• Cuts ruffled potato slices.
• Cuts potatoes for french fries (requires a special blade).

MELON "V" AND "U" CUTTERS

• Cuts decorative edges on fruits and vegetables.
• Used as a garnishing tool.

MELON AND FOOD BALLER

• Cuts melons and other foods into round balls.
• Scoops and hollows-out shallow indentations in fruits and vegetables for filling and stuffing.
• Removes cores from apple and pear halves.
• Used as a garnishing tool.

MORTAR AND PESTLE

The mortar and pestle are probably among man's oldest tools.
• Crushes garlic, herbs, nuts and seeds.
• Makes poultry, seafood and meat pastes.
• Used to make pesto in the absence of a food processor or blender.

MUSHROOM FLUTER

• Used to flute mushrooms.
• Used to remove ¼-inch pieces of citrus peel.
• Used as a sculpturing tool for garnishing.

NEEDLES

LARDING
• Threads additional fat through meat that is very lean so that the meat will not dry out when cooked.

STUFFING
• Stuffs olives and small food items into roasts.

TRUSSING
• Used with butcher string to tie poultry into a compact shape for roasting.

PASTRY EQUIPMENT

PASTRY BLENDER
• Cuts shortening into dry ingredients.

PASTRY BRUSHES
(see Brushes)

PASTRY CRIMPER
• Crimps and cuts pastry and cookie dough.
• Cuts wavy-edged pastry strips for lattice-topped fruit pies.
• Crimps and cuts ravioli.

PASTRY CUTTERS
• Cuts circles of pastry and cookie dough for dumplings and turnovers. These usually come in sets of assorted sizes, some with scalloped edges.

PASTRY JAGGER
• Pinches and flutes edges of double-crust pies.

PASTRY WHEEL
• Cuts pastry and cookie dough.
• Used in candy and fancy pastry work to cut and trim fondant.
• Some pastry wheels have a fluted blade which cuts a wavy edge.

PIE WEIGHTS
• Prevents unfilled pie shell from shrinking as it bakes.

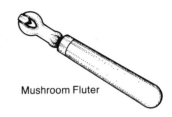

Mushroom Fluter

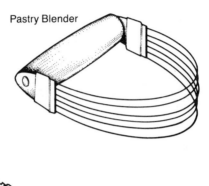

Pastry Blender

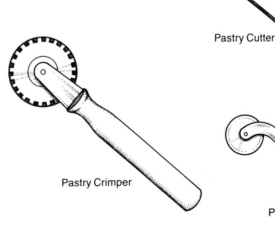

Pastry Cutter

Pastry Crimper

Pastry Wheel

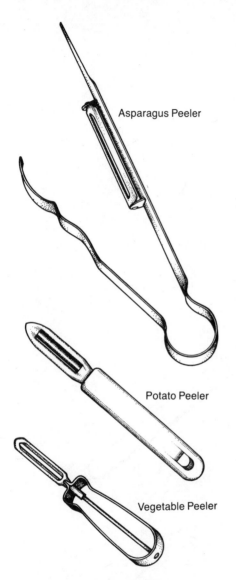

Asparagus Peeler

Potato Peeler

Vegetable Peeler

PEELERS

ASPARAGUS
• Trims the thick ends from asparagus stalks. This tool has an angled attachment that may be adjusted to the desired depth of trimming. The attachment may be removed and the tool used as a vegetable knife.

POTATO
(English Peeler)
• Peels potatoes, carrots, apples and other fruits and vegetables.
• Removes blemishes and bad spots from fruits and vegetables.
• Removes cores from apples and pears.

VEGETABLE
• Peels potatoes, cucumbers, carrots, celery, apples and other fruits and vegetables.
• Cuts thin, lengthwise strips of carrots for carrot curls.
• Shaves chocolate for chocolate curls.

PITTERS
FRUIT STONE REMOVERS

AVOCADO PITTER
• Removes avocado pits.

CHERRY-OLIVE PITTER
• Removes pits from cherries and olives.

FRUIT STONE REMOVER
• Removes pits from nectarines, peaches and plums.
• Scoops and hollows-out larger vegetables.

PIZZA CUTTER

• Cuts pizza into sections.
• Cuts sheet cakes and bar cookies.
• Cuts pastries.
• Used in candy making and pastry work to cut and trim fondant.

ROLLING PINS

BALL BEARING
This rolling pin moves smoothly across the pastry dough and assures even rolling with little tearing. Beginners will usually have the best luck using a pastry stocking on this rolling pin when rolling out pie pastry and some cookie doughs.

COPPER TUBE
This rolling pin consists of a solid tube of copper with fused wooden

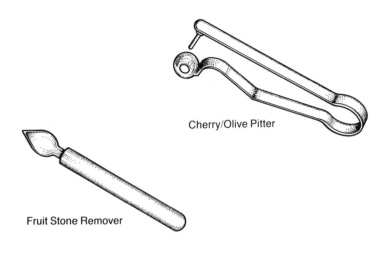

Cherry/Olive Pitter

Fruit Stone Remover

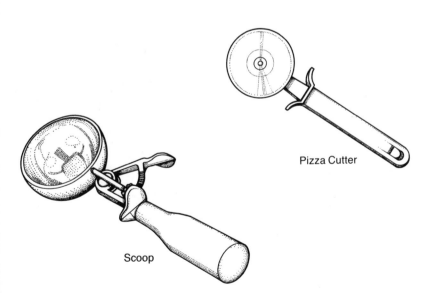

Scoop

Pizza Cutter

handles. It can be placed in the refrigerator and chilled for fancy pastry work.

FRENCH
This rolling pin is long and thin, often with tapering ends, and has no designated handles. It is preferred by many French chefs, but requires practice to learn to use it properly.

MARBLE
Like the copper tube, this rolling pin can be chilled for working with puff pastry and other pastry doughs. It is very heavy.

TUTOVE GROOVED
This rolling pin is specifically designed to use in puff pastry work. The grooves beat the pastry to soften the butter, and distribute the butter more evenly.

SCOOPS

There are regular scoops and paddles, most often used to serve iced desserts, and spring release scoops, suitable for other foods.

• Scoops ice creams, sherbets, and sorbets, cooked vegetable purees and mashed potatoes, some salads.

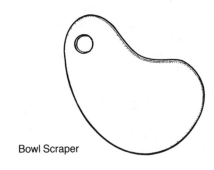

Bowl Scraper

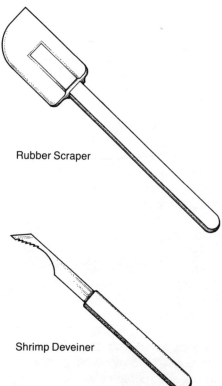

Rubber Scraper

Shrimp Deveiner

SCRAPERS

BOWL SCRAPER
• This flexible piece of plastic is used to scrape the sides of a bowl.

PASTRY SCRAPER
• Made of rigid metal with a plastic handle, this tool is used to scrape and lift yeast doughs, particularly brioche dough.
• Used in fancy pastry work to scrape and lift melted and slightly hardened chocolate. The chocolate is formed into strips for wrapping cakes or fashioned into large flowers.
• Used to cut dough when making loaves or rolls.
• Used to fold and mold fondant.

RUBBER SCRAPER
(Rubber Spatula)
• Folds and combines ingredients (especially egg whites) when gentle mixing is needed.
• Scrapes sides of mixing bowl when preparing doughs and batters.
• Scrapes containers clean.

SHRIMP DEVEINER

• Cuts through the shell and deveins the shrimp in one operation.

SIFTERS

CRANK
This sifter has one sifting screen and a hand-turned crank.

SPRING
A handle spring-activates the sifting mechanism. The spring mechanism often wears out or sticks.

ELECTRIC
A battery powers this motor-driven sifter.

Egg-Mushroom Slicer

Photograph: Molded Shellfish with scored cucumber rounds.

SLOTTED SPOONS AND SKIMMERS

• Removes foods from liquids, including hot fat; lets liquid drain away.
• A wire mesh skimmer works especially well to remove batter-coated foods from hot fat.

SLICERS

EGG-MUSHROOM
• Slices hardcooked eggs for garnishes and salads.
• Slices firm mushrooms.

TOMATO
• Slices firm tomatoes.

TRUFFLE
This tool does exist for those who have the budget to afford truffles. It has an adjustable blade somewhat like a mandoline.
• Cuts truffles, cheese and chocolate.

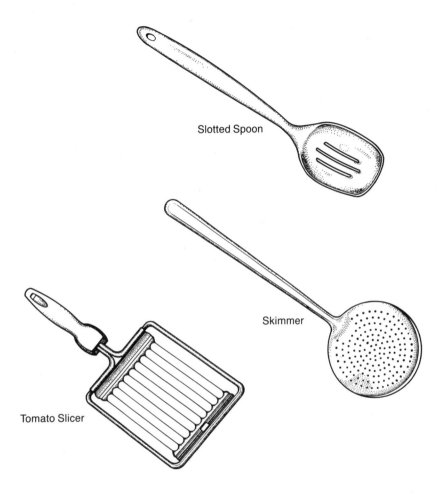

Slotted Spoon

Skimmer

Tomato Slicer

Truffle Slicer

Photograph: Rack of Lamb with tomato peel roses.

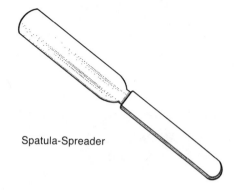

Spatula-Spreader

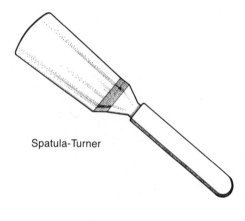

Spatula-Turner

Strawberry Huller

SPATULAS-SPREADERS

• Used to spread fillings and frostings.
• Used to level all measured dry ingredients. Flour should be sifted directly over a measuring cup, or sifted onto waxed paper and lightly spooned into the measuring cup, and then leveled with a quick straight-across motion using a spatula.
• Use spatulas with a serrated edge for slicing light, airy breads, and to achieve a "combed" look on frostings.

SPATULA-TURNERS

• Lifts and turns fried and grilled foods.
• The perforated spatula lifts fish from oil and poaching liquids.
• The Chinese spatula-turner is used in combination with a ladle to turn and fry foods in the wok.

STRAWBERRY HULLER

• Used like a tweezer to remove strawberry stems.
• Used like a tweezer to remove fish bones.

TEA BALL
SPICE INFUSER

• Holds whole spices and herbs used to flavor stocks, soups, stews, and punches. The seasonings are contained within the infuser which is removed before serving.

THERMOMETERS

Thermometers ensure accuracy and greater control over the cooking process. They are particularly helpful for candy making, roasting and preparation of yeast doughs.

CANDY—DEEP FRY
• Used in making candy to accurately determine the various stages of sugar syrup (soft and hard ball, soft and hard crack).
• Used in deep frying to accurately determine the temperature of the oil or shortening.

INSTANT READ
(Instant Response)
• Provides an almost immediate reading of internal temperature when inserted into food. Not left in during cooking.

MEAT
• Used when roasting meats and poultry to gauge internal temperature. Left in during cooking.

OVEN, REFRIGERATOR, FREEZER
• These thermometers check the temperature of their corresponding appliances. Quality is maintained when food is cooked or stored at proper temperature.

YEAST
• Provides a reading of the temperature of liquids used to prepare yeast doughs. Yeast is a living organism and must have the proper temperature to insure growth.

TOMATO PUREER

• Separates tomato pulp from skin and seeds, and purees pulp. This device is a boon to anyone preparing a great quantity of puree.

TONGS

• Lifts and turns fried and grilled foods. Tongs are preferred to a fork which can pierce and release juices, making meats tough and dry.

WHISKS

Many of the tasks formerly performed by whisks have been taken over by electric mixers and food processors. However, in classic French kitchens whisks are still the tool of choice.

FLAT
• Used to beat and mix eggs in a shallow dish or a plate.
• Used to whisk and mix in a shallow pan.

WIRE: BALLOON
• When used with a copper bowl to beat egg whites, this combination will yield maximum volume and will produce the finest and most stable foam.

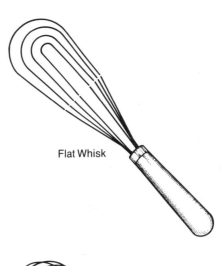
Flat Whisk

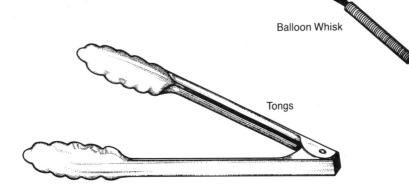
Balloon Whisk

Tongs

WIRE: FINE GAUGE
• Used to mix and blend light sauces and gravies.
• Used (in the absence of a balloon whisk) to whip egg whites.
• Used to whisk and combine salad dressings.
• Used (in the absence of a flour sifter) to stir and incorporate air into flour before measuring.

WIRE: HEAVY GAUGE
• Used to mix and blend heavy sauces.
• Used to mix and blend heavy batters.

WOODEN SPOONS AND SPATULAS

These are basic to any kitchen. They are recommended in most cases over metal spoons, as they treat food gently and won't react with food.

GENERAL PURPOSE
• Stirs flour mixtures in the preparation of doughs and batters.
• Stirs fruits and vegetables (less bruising).
• Used for sauces that require constant stirring over a long period of time.

ANGLED
• Used in steeply-angled saucepans.

EGG-LIFTING
• Lifts eggs in and out of boiling water.

SPAGHETTI FORK
• Stirs, lifts and separates pasta.

FLAT-EDGED
• Used in pairs for stir-frying.

ZESTER
(See Lemon Zester)

• Cuts long, fine pieces of citrus zest (the outer colored layer of the peel).

THESE FOOD PREPARATION techniques have been chosen because they clarify the use of the kitchen tools described in the previous section, are techniques called for in the recipes that follow or are those I find most often requested by students in my foods classes.

I am always aware of the visual and sensory appeal of creatively prepared and presented foods. Therefore, some simple, artistic garnishing techniques are also included.

techniques

Beet-Potato Shell

Cucumber Shell

Mushroom Shell

APPETIZER SHELLS

COOKED BABY BEET AND BABY NEW POTATO

Tools: Melon Baller

1. With small melon baller, scoop an indentation in beet or potato.
2. Fill hollowed-out vegetables with assorted cheese spreads and fish or chicken salad fillings. (The meat in the fillings should be finely diced.)

CUCUMBER

Tools: Fork or Mushroom Fluter, Utility Knife and Melon Baller, or Tomato Corer

1. Score cucumber with fork or mushroom fluter.
2. With utility knife, slice cucumber into ½-inch rounds.
3. Carefully scoop indentation with melon baller or tomato corer. Shell should be about ½-inch thick on the outer edge tapering to ⅛-inch in the center.

MUSHROOM

Tools: Melon Baller or Tomato Corer

1. Pull away stem.
2. Scoop indentation with melon baller or tomato corer.

CHERRY TOMATO

Tools: Small Melon Baller or Tomato Corer
Buy the largest and firmest cherry tomatoes.

1. Remove green stem. With serrated fruit or paring or utility knife, remove a small slice from top of cherry tomato.
2. Scoop out seeds and pulp with small melon baller or tomato corer.

SQUASH SHELL

Tools: Utility Knife or Chef's Knife, Melon Baller
Use large zucchini or crookneck squash. Large squash may be difficult to find in the market as they are considered too mature. Home gardeners can let some squash "overgrow" specifically for use as containers.

1. With utility or chef's knife, cut squash in half lengthwise.
2. With melon baller, scoop and remove seeds and some of the flesh from the squash half.

Cherry Tomato Shell

RED CABBAGE SHELL

Tools: Slicing or Chef's Knife, Grapefruit Knife, Melon Baller Use a firm and fairly good-sized cabbage.

1. With slicing or chef's knife, remove a thin slice from bottom of cabbage, if needed, so cabbage will sit upright.
2. Cut straight across one inch down from top of cabbage and remove top.
3. With grapefruit knife, cut around inside of cabbage, leaving a ½-inch rim.
4. Remove inner cabbage flesh with a large spoon. The melon baller can be used to further cut, scrape and hollow out the cabbage.

NOTE This hollowed-out cabbage is a fresh and festive container for dips. Place in a lettuce-lined basket with fancy crudités. This presentation makes an attractive centerpiece.

PINEAPPLE BOATS

Tools: Slicing Knife or Chef's Knife (8-inch), Grapefruit Knife.

1. With slicing or chef's knife, cut pineapple in half lengthwise (including green top). Cut each half into two quarter sections.
2. Remove fruit from the shell with a grapefruit knife.

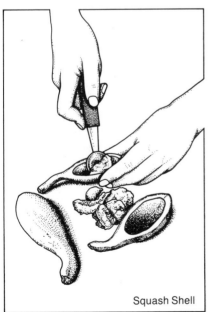

Squash Shell

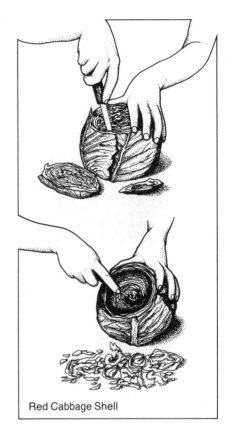

Red Cabbage Shell

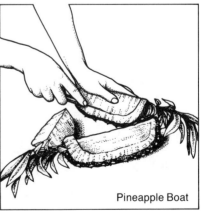

Pineapple Boat

TECHNIQUES 31

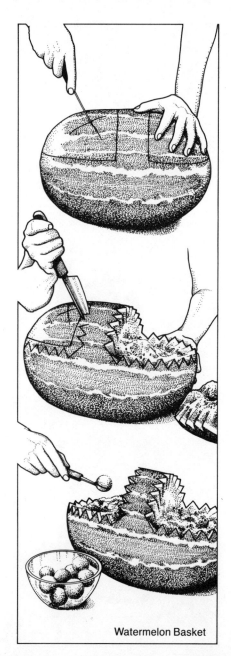

WATERMELON BASKET

Tools: Slicing Knife (8-inch), Melon "V" or "U" Cutter, Melon Baller Use a melon with a flat bottom, if possible.

1. If watermelon will not sit flat, remove a thin slice as needed from the bottom with slicing knife. Do not make too deep a cut.
2. Draw a handle across the top center of the melon, and then a horizontal line around the middle of the melon.
3. Cut an "x" in one of the side areas that are to be removed. (This will relieve any pressure and will keep melon from splitting.)
4. Push the melon "V" or "U" cutter into the melon along the drawn lines. When line is completely cut, remove the watermelon sections. sections.
5. Remove the red flesh of the watermelon, leaving a shell. If desired, use the melon baller to remove the flesh and make melon balls at the same time.

CITRUS BASKETS

Tools: Paring Knife, Grapefruit Knife, Melon Baller or Tomato Corer

1. With paring knife, cut sections from either side of the upper half of the fruit. Leave a ¼-inch strip across the top to form a handle.
2. Cut fruit along the rim with a grapefruit knife and remove pulp. Use a melon baller or tomato corer to ream out any additional pulp.

TOMATO TULIP BASKET

Tools: Curved Paring Knife or Serrated Fruit Knife, Melon Baller or Tomato Corer Use large, firm tomatoes.

1. Place tomato, stem end down, on a flat surface. With curved paring knife or serrated fruit knife, make 3 cuts across the top, cutting into the flesh slightly.
2. Peel back the petals, using knife to cut and lift each petal section.
3. To form container, remove seeds and most of pulp with melon baller or tomato corer, leaving a basket.

Watermelon Basket

Citrus Basket

RADISH ROSES

Tools: Paring Knife or Curved Paring Knife
You can vary the shape of the roses by purchasing plump round radishes and long slender radishes.

1. With paring knife, carefully cut five overlapping, even petals, rotating radish.
2. Place radishes in cold water for two hours to open up.

TOMATO ROSE

Tools: Sharp Curved Paring Knife or Paring Knife
Use firm tomatoes. If you have homegrown tomatoes, pick some while they are still ripening and are partially yellow-red. The resulting tomato rose will have a shaded effect.

1. With sharp paring knife remove peel in one long, continuous, ½-inch-wide strip.
2. Roll the tomato peel into a spiral to form a tomato rose.

NOTE This is an attractive garnish to use on buffet platters and on serving dishes for roasts and whole fish. For individual servings of salads, I have garnished with roses made from the large cherry tomatoes.

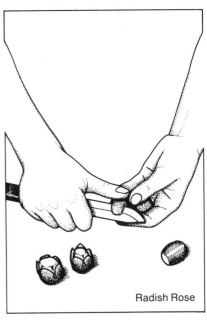

Radish Rose

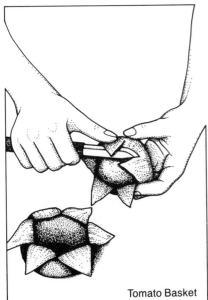

Tomato Basket

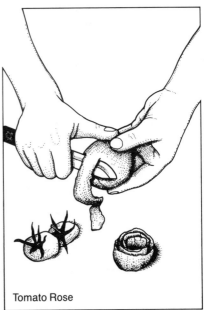

Tomato Rose

TECHNIQUES 33

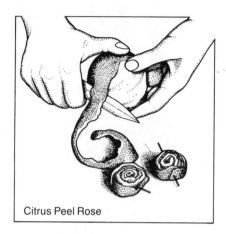
Citrus Peel Rose

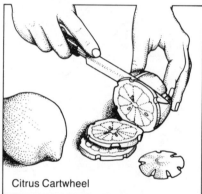
Citrus Cartwheel

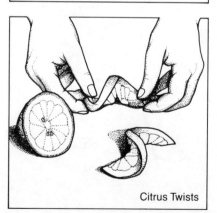
Citrus Twists

CITRUS PEEL ROSES

Tools: Curved Paring Knife or Paring Knife
You will also need toothpicks.

1. With curved paring knife cut one continuous strip of peel, slowly rotating fruit.
2. Twist and roll up peel to form a rose.
3. Secure with a toothpick.
4. Place in cold salted water and refrigerate for 4 hours. Drain well and pat dry before using as a garnish.

CITRUS CARTWHEELS

Tools: Citrus Stripper/Peeler or Mushroom Fluter, Utility Knife

1. Score citrus with stripper or fluter.
2. With utility knife, cut crosswise into slices.

CITRUS TWISTS

Tools: Utility Knife

1. Slice fruit into ¼-inch rounds.
2. Make one cut from center to edge of each slice.
3. Twist.

BELL PEPPER AND CHILE PEPPER FLOWERS

Tools: Curved Paring Knife
Use firm bell peppers in interesting shapes.

1. With paring knife, cut five petals in the pepper by cutting from the top tip of the pepper to within ½ inch of stem end.
2. For variation, pare and round each petal tip.
3. Place peppers in water and refrigerate overnight. The peppers will bloom.

NOTE You can make beautiful edible bouquets with fresh green leaves (kumquat, camelia, aralia), and flowers made from bell peppers, fluted mushrooms, radish roses, kumquat flowers and wooden skewers for stems. Use a piece of green onion stem to conceal the skewer.

CARROT-FLOWER COINS

Tools: Vegetable Peeler, Mushroom Fluter or Paring Knife

1. Peel carrot with vegetable peeler. With mushroom fluter or paring knife cut lengthwise grooves.
2. Cut carrot crosswise into ⅛- to ¼-inch slices.

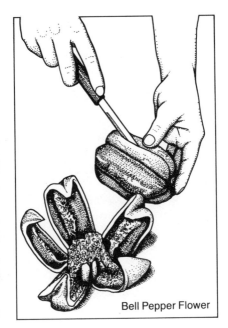

Bell Pepper Flower

KUMQUAT FLOWERS

Tools: Curved Paring Knife

1. With curved paring knife cut a five-point star through peel on rounded end of kumquat.
2. Carefully lift and peel away star from flesh. Remove star.
3. Carefully peel back points to form large flower.

NOTE You will have two garnishes—the flower and the peel stars.

CITRUS ZEST

Tools: Grater, or Zester and Kitchen Scissors, or Zester and Chef's Knife

METHOD 1
(Very fine, small pieces of zest)
1. With lemon grater or fine side of box grater, grate fruit, taking care to remove only the colored part of the peel.

METHOD 2
(Varying sizes of zest)
1. Hold fruit in one hand. Position thumb of other hand at the bottom of the fruit and draw the zester down from top to bottom.
2. Cut long strips of zest into shorter pieces with kitchen scissors, or chop with chef's knife.

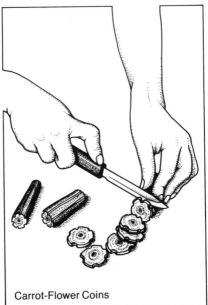

Carrot-Flower Coins

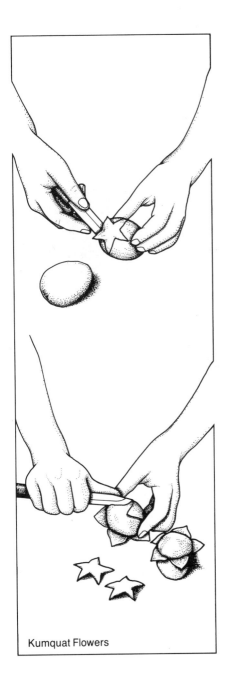

Kumquat Flowers

Radish Fan

Green Onion Fan

RADISH FANS

Tools: Curved Paring Knife or Paring Knife
Buy radishes that are blemish free with pretty leaves.

1. With knife, cut off root and a thin ($\frac{1}{16}$ inch) slice off tip.
2. Cut the radish lengthwise, making as many thin slices as possible.
3. Fan out the radish slices. The radishes can be soaked in cold water for 2 hours to bloom. (Immerse only the radish, not the leaves, in the cold water.)

GREEN ONION FANS

Tools: Sharp Paring Knife
Use green onions that are somewhat plump. You can make short fans using only the white part of the onion, or you can make longer fans by leaving some of the green tops on.

1. Slice off the root tip with knife.
2. Make as many lengthwise sliver cuts in white part of onion as possible.
3. Place cut fans in ice water for 2 hours; they will curl and bloom.

MELON AND FOOD BALLS

Tools: Melon or Food Baller
Melons should be ripe but still somewhat firm.

1. With rounded side of melon baller facing up, press tool into flesh of fruit or vegetable.
2. Push inward, and twist and rotate tool.
3. Lift up with ball of food right side up.

FLUTING MUSHROOMS

Tools: Mushroom Fluter, Citrus Stripper/Peeler or Small Paring Knife

METHOD 1
(Fluter/Stripper)
1. Hold mushroom with one hand.
2. With other hand, starting at center of the top of the mushroom, score the cap with the cutting edge of fluter at even intervals.

METHOD 2
(Knife)
1. Slice "v" shaped sections into mushroom cap with small paring knife.
2. With the point of the knife starting at the center of the top of the mushroom, remove the sections.
3. Slice across the bottom of the mushroom to remove any trimmings.

Melon Balls

SCORED CUCUMBER SLICES

Tools: Vegetable Peeler, Fork or Mushroom Fluter, Utility Knife

1. Peel cucumber, if desired, with a vegetable peeler.
2. Score cucumber with fork or mushroom fluter.
3. Cut crosswise into desired width slices with utility knife.

CUCUMBER CRESCENTS

Tools: Vegetable Peeler, Utility Knife, Melon Baller or Tomato Corer

1. Peel cucumber with vegetable peeler.
2. Cut cucumber in half lengthwise with utility knife.
3. Scoop out seeds with melon baller or tomato corer.
4. With utility knife, cut crosswise into ¼-inch slices.

CHOCOLATE LEAVES

Tools: Small Metal Spatula
You will need camellia or gardenia leaves that are clean and have not been sprayed with insecticides, and semisweet chocolate or chocolate chips

1. Melt chocolate over hot water in a double boiler. Spread melted chocolate on the underside of the leaves with a spatula, being careful to come just to the edge. Place leaves on plate or cookie sheet and chill.
2. Carefully peel green leaves from chocolate. Chocolate leaves may be placed in a sturdy container and frozen.

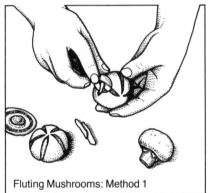

Fluting Mushrooms: Method 1

Fluting Mushrooms: Method 2

Scored Cucumber Slices

Chocolate Leaves

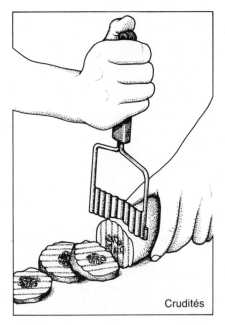

Crudités

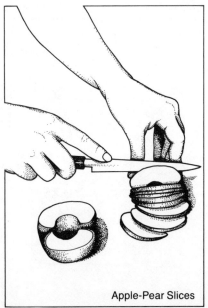

Apple-Pear Slices

CRUDITES

Tools: Crinkle Chip Cutter, Curved Paring Knife or Vegetable Peeler
Use firm vegetables such as carrots, jícama, squash and cucumber.

1. Peel vegetables, if necessary, with curved paring knife or vegetable peeler.
2. With crinkle chip cutter, cut cucumbers and some of the squash in round chips.
3. With crinkle chip cutter, cut carrots, jícama and some of the squash in wavy sticks.

THIN APPLE AND PEAR SLICES FOR TARTS AND PASTRIES

Tools: Vegetable Peeler, Utility or Fruit Knife, Melon Baller
This method makes the center cut rounded and smooth and with a minimum loss of edible fruit.

1. Peel apple or pear with a vegetable peeler.
2. With knife, cut in half lengthwise.
3. With melon baller, cut and remove core.
4. Place apple or pear half on a cutting surface, flat side down; slice thinly and evenly with knife.

CHOCOLATE CURLS

Tools: Vegetable Peeler, or Knife and Marble Slab

METHOD 1
(Vegetable Peeler)
1. Shave chocolate block (chocolate should be at room temperature) with a sharp vegetable peeler.

METHOD 2
(Knife and Marble Slab)
1. Melt chocolate; spread on marble slab. Place in refrigerator to firm. Draw a knife edge across the chocolate to form large curls.

PEELING AND SECTIONING CITRUS FRUIT

Tools: Paring Knife or Fruit Knife

1. With a paring or fruit knife, remove peel and white membrane while rotating fruit.
2. Cut between pulp and membrane of each section. Fruit will easily slip out.

SHUCKING OYSTERS

Tools: Oyster Knife

1. Hold oyster knife in writing hand.
2. Hold oyster tightly in opposite hand with rounded side down (to catch liquor).
3. Insert end of knife between shells near hinge and twist to pry open. Work knife blade around shells to sever hinge.
4. Work knife blade around oyster to release. Save oyster liquor for use as flavor enhancer in sauces, or if eating oyster raw, drink liquor and oyster directly from shell.

DEVEINING AND SHELLING SHRIMP

Tools: Shrimp Deveiner or Small Paring Knife.

METHOD 1
(Shrimp Deveiner)
1. Remove heads from shrimp if still on.
2. Hold shrimp in its natural curve with tail down. Insert deveiner (cutting edge up, notched edge down) under the shell along the back. Push toward the tail, cutting the shell until the blade reaches tail's end (the notched teeth of the deveiner will clean out the vein).
3. Remove the shrimp from its shell and wash under cold water to remove any traces of the vein.

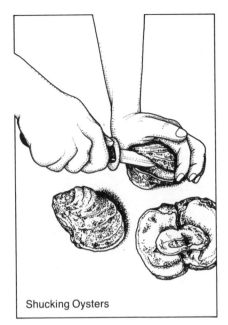

Shucking Oysters

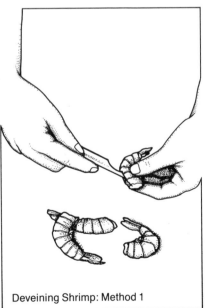

Deveining Shrimp: Method 1

METHOD 2
(Paring Knife)
1. With knife, cut through the shell on the outer curved edge; remove shell.
2. With knife, slit open the curved back side of the shrimp and scrape and remove intestinal vein. Rinse shrimp with cold water to remove any remaining vein.

TRUSSING A CHICKEN, TURKEY OR DUCK

Tools: Trussing Needle and Butcher String
Trussing keeps the bird compact and attractive.

1. Thread needle. Insert needle through the lower part of the carcass.
2. Bring string over one drumstick. Insert needle through breast bone tip and then bring string over the second drumstick; tie securely.
3. Insert needle through upper part of thigh of one leg, then through carcass and out through other thigh.
4. Fold wings back. Turn chicken on breast. Insert needle through one wing, catch the neck skin against the backbone and come out the other wing; tie string tight.

BONING CHICKEN

Tools: Paring Knife or Boning Knife, Poultry Shears or Kitchen Scissors

BONING A CHICKEN BREAST HALF

1. Place chicken breast on board. Begin at pointed end of breast and insert knife along breast bone. Cut meat away from bone with knife edge flat against breast bone. Lift flesh and gently pull as you cut.
2. Remove tendon from breast.

BONING A WHOLE CHICKEN, DUCK, OR TURKEY

Tool: Small Paring Knife, Kitchen Scissors

1 Place chicken, breast side down, on a flat surface. With knife, cut through skin along backbone. With knife, scrape down backbone, gently lifting flesh away.
2. Disjoint thigh and wing bones from carcass with poultry shears or kitchen scissors. Scrape meat from thigh and upper wing bone. Disjoint the thigh bone and the upper wing bone; discard. Repeat this procedure for other side. Carefully cut flesh from breast bone with knife. Be careful not to pierce the skin.*

*The chicken can be stuffed at this point and sewed up. The lower wing and leg bones can be left, thus making the boned chicken still resemble a bird. If you wish to do a stuffed chicken terrine or a gallantine you can further scrape the meat from these bones and remove the bones entirely.

CHOPPING, DICING AND MINCING

There are several ways to chop, dice and mince ingredients—with a knife, bowl chopper, mincer, food processor. When deciding which method to use consider quantity and cleanup. For small quantities most cooks can chop with and clean a cutting board and chef's knife quicker than if using a mincer or the food processor. For large quantities, the food processor is ideal.

The following is offered as a visual guide to size designations commonly used in most recipes.

Finest Minced: Garlic Press

Minced

Finely Diced

Diced

Chopped

Rough Chopped

Julienne Cut

ROLLING PASTRY

Tools: Rolling Pin
Beginners may wish to work with a pastry cloth and a stocking for the rolling pin.

1. Form mixed pastry into ball and flatten slightly. Wrap in plastic and refrigerate 30 minutes.
2. Transfer chilled dough to lightly floured surface. Roll pastry into a circle, using several rolling motions beginning in the center and rolling outwards.
3. Roll dough around rolling pin. Place pin over pie dish and then unroll pastry slowly. Fit dough into dish without stretching the dough.
4. Trim edges 1 inch beyond edge of dish. Moisten rim with water. Turn in pastry and flute edges.

FOUR STAGES OF WHISKED OR BEATEN EGG WHITES

For soufflés it is better to slightly underbeat than overbeat egg whites. Overbeaten egg whites cannot be properly incorporated. The most ideal egg white foam is obtained with a copper bowl and wire whisk. The wire whisk produces a more stable foam with smaller bubbles, which in turn gives greater volume to a baked product.

The following terms are commonly used to describe the different stages of beaten egg whites.

FOAMY Egg whites are slightly beaten. Salt or cream of tartar is added at this stage if called for in the recipe.

SOFT PEAKS Beaten egg whites begin to form peaks which bend over.

STIFF, BUT NOT DRY Beaten egg whites stand in stiff peaks. If bowl is tipped, egg whites will not slide.

DRY Egg whites are overbeaten. The whites separate into dry curds and liquid.

FOLDING

Tools: Rubber Spatula (Scraper)
Folding is a common technique in both basic and advanced food preparation. It's best done with a rubber spatula. The motion of folding is one of cutting and lifting rather than stirring. For soufflés, the base (thickened, flavored white sauce) should first be lightened. To lighten the base, add ⅓ of the beaten egg whites to the base and mix in. You do not have to fold or use care for this. Then fold the base into the beaten egg whites, using the folding technique.

1. Cut down with the spatula, turning the wrist.
2. Lift up with the spatula, then fold over and repeat cutting, lifting and turning until the ingredients are blended.
3. Turn the bowl around as you work.

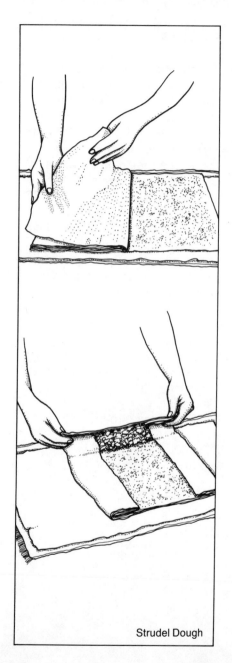

Strudel Dough

SHAPING AND FORMING STRUDELS

EQUIPMENT:
1 large tea towel, dampened
1 sheet waxed paper cut the width of the tea towel
Wide pastry brush

INGREDIENTS
Filo leaves: 4 to 6 for dessert strudels and 6 to 8 for main dish strudels
¾ cup to 1 cup melted unsalted butter per large strudel
¼ to ½ cup bread crumbs per strudel

1. Place tea towel on large surface; cover towel with waxed paper.
2. Lay filo on top of waxed paper. Pretend the filo is a book and close the book (leave waxed paper and towel open).
3. Open the first leaf, brush with melted butter and sprinkle with bread crumbs. (You are covering half of the filo leaf with the butter and bread crumbs.)
4. Continue buttering the filo and sprinkling with bread crumbs until you reach the middle of the book. Close the book to the left. Open one page and butter and spread crumbs on this section of filo leaves, until the center is reached. Butter the center leaf.
5. Spread strudel filling on lower end of filo, leaving a one-inch border.
6. Fold in side edges.
7. Lift towel and flip strudel over and over, forming a nice tight roll.

BAKING Place strudel on jelly-roll pan (with raised sides). Brush with melted butter. Bake in 375°F. oven for ten minutes, then remove and cut slices two-thirds through with a serrated knife. Brush with melted butter and return strudel to oven and bake an additional 15 to 25 minutes until nicely browned and cooked through.

MY CLASSES AND RECIPES
reflect today's emphasis on the use
of the freshest and finest ingredients, lighter sauces, grilling and
the influence of many cultures. The
visual and artistic presentation of
food is an important element of this
new style, and an important part of
my own food philosophy. I have always considered cooking both sci-
ence and art and have depended
upon my collection of kitchen tools
and equipment as an artist turns to
his brush or palette knife. These
tools will always be needed for
many of the precise, skilled tasks of
food preparation.

appetizers

HERBED SPINACH CREAM

1 package (10 ounces) frozen
    chopped spinach, or 1 large
    bunch (about ¾ pound) fresh
    spinach, rinsed, stemmed and
    finely chopped
1 cup sour cream
⅓ cup mayonnaise
⅓ cup minced fresh parsley
3 tablespoons minced fresh chives
2 tablespoons minced green onions
2 teaspoons minced fresh dill
½ teaspoon celery salt
A hollowed-out red cabbage for ac-
    companiment (page 31)
Assorted chilled crudités for ac-
    companiment (page 38)

In a medium saucepan bring ½ cup
water to boiling. Add frozen or fresh
spinach and cook for 2 minutes, or
until tender; drain thoroughly.
Squeeze out all moisture. If using
frozen spinach, chop the cooked
spinach into finer pieces; set aside.
In a large bowl combine the sour
cream, mayonnaise, parsley,
chives, green onions, dill and celery
salt; add the spinach and combine.
Cover and refrigerate for several
hours to blend flavors. To serve,
spoon chilled dip into the hollowed-
out cabbage; arrange cabbage and
assorted chilled crudités in a decorative basket. Makes 2 cups dip.

BROCCOLI, CARROTS AND SNOW PEAS WITH WATERCRESS DIP

1 bunch broccoli
1 pound snow peas, strings
    removed
6 to 8 medium carrots, cut in finger-
    sized pieces, or several bunches
    of tiny carrots
Watercress Dip (following)

Cut the flowerets from the bunch of
broccoli; reserve stems for another
use. Cook flowerets in boiling,
salted water until bright green and
crisp-tender. Blanch snow peas in
boiling water until bright green and
crisp-tender, 1 to 2 minutes, or microwave at high power 45 seconds,
or until bright green and crisp-tender. Cook carrots until crisp-tender.
Arrange the cooked vegetables in
an attractive pattern on a tray or
serving platter. Chill.
   Serve chilled vegetables with
Watercress Dip. Makes 8 to 10
servings.

WATERCRESS DIP In a food processor or blender puree ¾ cup
packed watercress leaves, ½ cup
mayonnaise, ½ cup sour cream, 2
tablespoons chopped fresh parsley,
1 tablespoon minced onion, 1 clove
pressed garlic and ½ teaspoon celery salt. Makes 1¼ cups.

SALSA PICANTE DIP

1 package (8 ounces) cream
    cheese, softened
½ cup Salsa Supreme (page 124)
⅓ cup finely chopped fresh cilantro
    leaves
2 tablespoons grated onion
1 large clove garlic, pressed
2 teaspoons fresh lemon juice
Dash of ground cinnamon
Dash of ground cloves
¼ teaspoon salt (optional)
Assorted fresh crudités (page 38),
    or 1 pound medium cooked
    shrimp for accompaniment

In a food processor or blender puree cream cheese, salsa, cilantro,
onion, garlic, lemon juice, cinnamon, cloves and salt. Serve with a
variety of fresh crudités or cooked
shrimp. Makes 1¾ cups dip.

NOTE Salsa Picante Dip also
makes an excellent topping for barbecued or grilled fish.

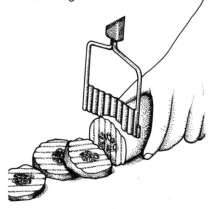

TEX-MEX DIP

3 medium ripe avocados
2 tablespoons fresh lemon juice
½ teaspoon salt
¼ teaspoon freshly ground black
    pepper
1 cup sour cream
½ cup mayonnaise
1 small clove garlic, pressed
1½ teaspoons chili powder
¼ teaspoon paprika
2 cups jalapeño refried beans (1
    15-ounce can refried beans
    mixed with 4 tablespoons salsa
    and 2 seeded and finely minced
    jalapeño peppers)
1 large bunch green onions with
    tops, chopped
3 medium tomatoes, cored, halved,
    seeded and coarsely chopped
1 can (8 ounces) pitted ripe olives,
    drained and chopped
8 ounces Cheddar cheese, grated
2 packages large round tortilla
    chips for accompaniment

Peel, pit and mash avocados. Combine with lemon juice, salt and pepper. Combine sour cream, mayonnaise, garlic and seasonings.
Spread refried beans on a large
shallow serving platter, top with
seasoned avocado mixture and
then sour cream mixture. Sprinkle
with chopped green onions, tomatoes and olives; cover with grated
cheese. Serve with round tortilla
chips. Makes 16 to 20 servings.

BOURSIN CHEESE

1 package (8 ounces) cream
    cheese, softened
1 large clove garlic, pressed
1 teaspoon Morton's seasoning
    blend
2 tablespoons whipping cream
2 tablespoons minced fresh
    parsley, or 2 teaspoons freshly
    cracked black pepper
Crackers for accompaniment

In a food processor puree cream
cheese, garlic, seasoning and
cream; or combine in a large bowl
and beat with an electric mixer until
smooth. Line a 1-cup mold with
plastic wrap and pack cheese into
mold; refrigerate until firm, about 2
hours. Unmold onto a serving plate
and remove plastic wrap. Sprinkle
top of cheese with minced parsley
or cracked pepper. Serve with an
assortment of crackers. Makes 1
cup.

VARIATION With Endive: Add 1 to 2 tablespoons chopped fresh herbs (chervil, basil or thyme) and 2 tablespoons whipping cream to the cheese mixture (do not use parsley or pepper). For each serving, spoon about 1 teaspoon of the cheese mixture onto the large end of a Belgian endive leaf (buy 3 to 4 heads endive). Garnish with fresh alfalfa sprouts. Makes 24 to 30 appetizers.

With Smoked Salmon in Cucumber Cups: Score 2 hothouse cucumbers with a mushroom fluter or fork; slice into ½-inch rounds. With a melon baller cut a shallow cup in one end of each cucumber round. Wrap slices in paper towels and refrigerate several hours to remove excess moisture. To serve, fill each cucumber slice with Boursin cheese. Place ¼- by 1-inch strips of Nova Scotia lox (buy ¼ pound lox) crosswise over cheese; garnish with fresh dill sprigs. Arrange on a serving platter, cover and refrigerate up to 2 hours until ready to serve. Makes 36 to 48 appetizers.

DRIED TOMATOES

3 pounds ripe Italian Roma tomatoes, washed
Salt
3 sprigs fresh rosemary
2 cups imported virgin olive oil

Slice tomatoes in half lengthwise. Using the melon baller scoop out pulp. Lay the tomatoes, cut side up and about 1 inch apart, either on dehydrator trays or on wire cooling racks set on cookie sheets; sprinkle lightly with salt.

For dehydrator: Place racks in dehydrator (125°F.) and dry until tomatoes are shriveled, but still flexible (not brittle), about 7 to 10 hours depending on size and thickness of tomato halves. (After 7 hours of drying, check hourly and remove those tomatoes that have dried.) Let cool.

For oven drying: Place cookie sheets with prepared tomato halves in 140°F. oven and dry until tomatoes are shriveled, but still flexible (not brittle). See Dehydrator method, but start to check after 4 hours.

Place dried tomato halves in a large mason jar or crock. Add the fresh rosemary sprigs and cover with olive oil. Makes about 6 ounces dried tomatoes.

NOTE Dried tomatoes should keep for 2 months. If mold develops on tomatoes, refrigerate. Allow tomatoes to return to room temperature before serving. Use dried tomatoes in appetizers, in antipasto platters, in salads, sprinkled over pizza, and in pasta sauces.

CHEVRE WITH DRIED TOMATOES

24 slices baguette
Reserved olive oil from marinated dried tomatoes
24 Dried Tomato halves (preceding)
4 ounces Bucheron chèvre*

With a pastry brush lightly brush the baguette slices with olive oil. Top each slice with a tomato half; cover each tomato half with a small piece of cheese. Place bread slices on a baking sheet; broil or bake until heated through and cheese is slightly melted. Makes 24 appetizers.

*Available at better cheese shops and some gourmet markets.

SKEWERED TORTELLINI WITH SPINACH-BASIL PESTO SAUCE

½ cup mayonnaise
½ cup sour cream
⅓ cup Spinach-Basil Pesto
  (following)
4 ounces prepared tortellini,
  cooked, drained and cooled
1 pint cherry tomatoes
Medium wooden skewers
Red leaf lettuce for garnish
A hollowed-out red cabbage (page
  31)

To prepare sauce combine mayonnaise, sour cream and Spinach-Basil Pesto in a medium bowl; cover and refrigerate. To serve, skewer cooked tortellini alternately with cherry tomatoes. Arrange filled skewers in a basket lined with red leaf lettuce. Accompany with Spinach-Basil Pesto Sauce in a hollowed-out red cabbage. Makes 1⅓ cups sauce and about 20 skewers.

SPINACH-BASIL PESTO In a food processor or blender puree 1¼ cups packed fresh spinach leaves, ½ cup Italian or regular parsley, ½ cup packed fresh basil leaves and 2 pressed cloves garlic; add ¾ cup freshly grated Parmesan cheese and ½ cup lightly toasted pine nuts (page 126) and process. With machine on, add ⅔ cup virgin olive oil in a slow, steady stream and process until smooth and creamy. To make with mortar and pestle, place pine nuts and garlic in mortar and grind with pestle. Add cheese and stir and grind. Add finely minced spinach leaves, basil and parsley to pine nut mixture. Slowly add oil, continuing to grind and stir with pestle. Makes 2½ cups.

PESTO-DRIED TOMATO TORTA

1 package (8 ounces) cream
  cheese, softened
¼ pound butter, softened
⅓ cup marinated Dried Tomatoes,
  drained and finely chopped
  (page 46)
½ cup Spinach-Basil Pesto
  (preceding)
1 head red leaf lettuce
1 small baguette, sliced

In a food processor puree cream cheese and butter; or, place in a medium bowl and beat with an electric mixer. Line a 2-cup mold with plastic wrap. Spread one-third of the cheese-butter mixture in bottom of mold. Cover with chopped tomatoes and then another one-third of the cheese-butter mixture, spreading evenly. Spread the pesto sauce over the cheese. Freeze about 15 to 20 minutes. Cover evenly with remaining cheese-butter mixture. Refrigerate at least 2 hours or overnight. Unmold onto serving dish or basket lined with red leaf lettuce; remove plastic wrap. Serve at room temperature on slices of baguette. Makes one 2-cup mold.

MOLDED SHELLFISH

12 ounces cooked shrimp or crab meat
2 hard-cooked eggs, peeled and chopped
½ cup stuffed green olives, sliced
2 tablespoons capers, rinsed and drained
1 tablespoon snipped fresh chives
1 envelope unflavored gelatin
¼ cup cold water
2 cups mayonnaise
Garnish: 1 head curly endive or red leaf lettuce, olive slices, pimiento pieces, and halved cucumber slices
Crackers, or 1 hothouse cucumber, scored with a mushroom fluter or fork and sliced into rounds, for accompaniment

Combine shellfish, eggs, olives, capers and chives; set aside. In a small saucepan soak gelatin in cold water 5 minutes, then dissolve gelatin mixture over very low heat. Add small amount of mayonnaise to gelatin, stirring constantly, then add this mixture to remaining mayonnaise. Blend mayonnaise mixture with fish mixture. Spoon into oiled 3-cup fish or ring mold and chill until firm. Arrange a bed of endive on a serving plate. Unmold appetizer onto the endive. Decorate the fish with sliced olives for eyes and pimiento for mouth. Arrange half-slices of cucumber to resemble fish scales. Serve on a buffet as a salad or accompany with crackers and cucumber rounds and serve as an appetizer. Makes 30 appetizer servings or 8 salad servings.

PINEAPPLE BOWLS WITH AMARETTO CREAM CHEESE

1 fresh pineapple, halved lengthwise (including green top)
2 packages (8 ounces each) cream cheese, softened
4 egg yolks
½ cup sugar
¼ cup Amaretto
1 tablespoon unflavored gelatin
¼ cup water
Endive or red leaf lettuce for garnish
Sliced pears and apples for accompaniment
Juice of 2 lemons

With grapefruit knife carve and remove flesh from pineapple halves. Reserve pineapple meat for another use or cut in cubes and serve with the molded cheese. Drain pineapple bowl upside down on paper towels. In a food processor or with an electric mixer cream cheese; add egg yolks, one at a time. Add sugar and Amaretto and beat until smooth. In a small saucepan soften gelatin in cold water for 5 minutes; dissolve gelatin by cooking briefly over low heat. Add 2 to 3 tablespoons of the cream cheese mixture to the warm gelatin; stir until smooth. With processor on, pour gelatin mixture through feed tube into work bowl and process until smooth. Pour into pineapple bowls. Cover with plastic wrap and refrigerate 4 hours. To serve, line a basket (bottom covered with plastic wrap) or a large platter with endive. Set filled pineapple bowls on greens. Surround with pear and apple slices which have been acidulated with lemon juice. Makes about 20 servings.

PECAN BAKED BRIE

1 whole, firm Brie (about 2 pounds)
2 tablespoons melted butter
2 tablespoons packed brown sugar
1 cup pecan halves
Apple wedges, bread sticks or crackers for accompaniment

Place the Brie in a 10-inch round baking dish; brush with 2 tablespoons melted butter. Force the brown sugar through a wire sieve onto the top of the cheese. Cover decoratively with pecan halves. Bake in a 350°F. oven until the cheese begins to melt, about 10 to 12 minutes. Keep warm on a warming tray. Scoop up with apple wedges, bread sticks or crackers. Makes about 25 appetizer servings.

TOMATO AND STILTON CHEESE TART

1 unbaked 10-inch pastry shell (use Double Crust Pastry, page 127)
Egg wash (1 egg beaten with 1 tablespoon cold water)
2 tablespoons minced shallots
2 medium tomatoes, peeled, thinly sliced and drained
12 ounces Stilton cheese, crumbled
4 eggs
1 pint whipping cream

Line pastry shell with aluminum foil and fill with beans or metal pie weights. Bake in a 400°F. oven for 15 minutes; remove foil and beans. Brush interior of shell with egg wash; bake 2 minutes more. Remove from oven. Distribute shallots and tomato slices in shell. Sprinkle cheese over tomato slices. Whisk eggs; add the cream and mix well. Strain into pie shell. Reduce oven temperature to 350°F. Bake 35 to 40 minutes, or until custard is set. Cool 20 minutes before serving. Makes 10 to 12 servings.

FLAN AU ROQUEFORT

4 ounces Roquefort cheese
4 eggs
1 pint whipping cream
1 teaspoon grated lemon peel
⅛ teaspoon white pepper
⅛ teaspoon paprika
Dash of freshly grated nutmeg

In a heavy-bottomed saucepan slowly melt the Roquefort cheese over very low heat. Whisk eggs lightly and add to the cheese. Whisk in the cream, lemon peel and seasonings; blend well. Pour into a well-greased 10-inch quiche dish. Place quiche dish in a baking pan with enough boiling water to come halfway up the sides of the quiche dish. Bake in a 400°F. oven 25 to 30 minutes, or until set. Makes 8 to 10 servings.

NOTE The flan may also be served as part of a dessert course. Accompany with fresh fruits such as apples, pears or peaches.

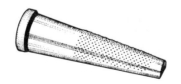

MARINATED SHRIMP AND PEA PODS

30 medium cooked shrimp, peeled and deveined
½ cup Lemon Vinaigrette (following)
30 snow peas, strings removed
Lettuce leaves for garnish

Marinate shrimp in vinaigrette for several hours. Blanch snow peas in boiling water until bright green and crisp-tender, 1 to 2 minutes, or microwave at high power 45 seconds until bright green and crisp-tender. Drain shrimp, reserving marinade. Wrap a snow pea around each shrimp and secure with toothpicks. Place in marinade and refrigerate up to 1 hour. Drain and serve in lettuce-lined dish, or basket lined with plastic wrap and lettuce. Makes 30 appetizers.

LEMON VINAIGRETTE In a medium bowl whisk together ½ cup olive oil, ⅓ cup lemon juice, ¼ cup snipped fresh chives, 1 tablespoon finely minced shallot, 1 teaspoon Dijon-style mustard and salt and freshly ground black pepper to taste.

CAPERED SHRIMP AND CHEESE

1½ cups water
1½ cups dry white wine
1 lemon, sliced
2 bay leaves
½ teaspoon black peppercorns
1 pounds medium raw shrimp
1 package (8 ounces) cream
    cheese, softened
3 anchovy fillets, rinsed
3 tablespoons butter, softened
1 tablespoon fresh lemon juice
1 teaspoon Dijon-style mustard
2 small green onions, minced
1 tablespoon capers, rinsed and
    drained
Salt and freshly ground black pep-
    per to taste
3 cucumbers, sliced into 50 rounds,
    or 50 cooked new potato halves,
    scooped out with melon baller,
    for accompaniment
1 bunch fresh dill for garnish

In a medium saucepan combine water, wine, lemon, bay leaves and black peppercorns and bring to boil over high heat. Cover, reduce heat to medium-low and simmer 10 minutes. Add shrimp and simmer 3 to 5 minutes; set aside to cool. Transfer shrimp in cooking liquid to another container, cover and chill overnight.

Drain shrimp well; remove shells and devein. In a food processor puree cream cheese, anchovies, butter, lemon juice and mustard. Add shrimp and process finely using on/off turns. Transfer to a bowl and blend in green onions, capers, salt and pepper. Cover and refrigerate overnight; or, place cream cheese, anchovies, butter, lemon juice and mustard in a large mixing bowl and beat with an electric mixer until smooth. Chop shrimp and add to cheese mixture with green onions, capers, salt and pepper; combine with a wooden spoon (do not use mixer or you will end up with shrimp paste). Cover and refrigerate overnight.

The spread may be packed in crocks, spread on cucumber rounds or used to fill scooped-out new potato halves. Garnish with fresh dill sprigs. Makes 50 appetizers.

SMOKED SALMON IN ARTICHOKE HEARTS

6 large artichokes
⅓ cup fresh lemon juice
6 ounces smoked salmon, minced
6 tablespoons mayonnaise
6 tablespoons sour cream
2 tablespoons minced fresh parsley
1 tablespoon grated onion
2 teaspoons snipped fresh dill
1 tablespoon capers, rinsed and
    drained
1 head butter lettuce, leaves sepa-
    rated, for garnish
Tomato roses for garnish (page 33)

Trim away artichoke leaves and reserve for another use. With melon baller remove choke from each artichoke to expose heart. Sprinkle hearts with lemon juice to prevent browning. Steam artichoke hearts until tender; chill. Combine salmon, mayonnaise, sour cream, parsley, onion, dill and capers in a small bowl and mix well. Spoon into artichoke hearts. To serve, arrange lettuce leaves on salad plates, top with artichoke hearts and garnish with small tomato roses. Makes 6 servings.

NOTE Filling may be prepared in advance and chilled. One hour before serving, spoon filling into artichokes; chill until ready to serve.

CAPONATA

½ cup olive oil
1 clove garlic
1 large eggplant, peeled and cut in
    1-inch cubes
2 onions, sliced
1 cup chopped celery
1 can (16 ounces) Italian-style to-
    matoes with juice, chopped fine
12 green olives, pitted
2 tablespoons capers
6 anchovy fillets, chopped
¼ cup wine vinegar
¼ cup dry red wine
2 tablespoons sugar
½ teaspoon salt
Pinch of freshly ground black
    pepper
Hollowed-out squash shell (op-
    tional, page 30)
1 baguette, sliced, or crackers

In a large skillet heat oil, add garlic and cook garlic several minutes to flavor oil; discard garlic. Add eggplant and cook until tender, about 8 to 10 minutes. Add onions and celery and sauté about 5 minutes. Stir in tomatoes and simmer about 15 minutes. Stir in olives, capers, anchovies, vinegar, wine, sugar, salt and pepper. Simmer 20 minutes, stirring occasionally. Cool and refrigerate, covered, up to 2 weeks. Serve chilled in a hollowed-out squash, if desired, with baguette slices or crackers. Makes 3 cups.

PICKLED MUSHROOMS

⅔ cup tarragon vinegar
½ cup vegetable oil
1 medium clove garlic, pressed
2 tablespoons water
1 tablespoon sugar
1 teaspoon salt
Dash of hot pepper sauce
1 medium white onion, sliced and
    separated into rings
1 pound small domestic mush-
    rooms, trimmed

Combine the vinegar, oil, garlic, water, sugar, salt and hot pepper sauce. Place onion rings and mushrooms in a bowl; add marinade. Cover and refrigerate at least 24 hours. Makes about 40 mushrooms.

STUFFED CHERRY TOMATOES

30 cherry tomatoes (about 1¼
    pints)
1 cup minced cooked ham, roast
    beef or shrimp
1 dill pickle, minced
2 to 3 tablespoons mayonnaise
1 tablespoon Dijon-style mustard
1 tablespoon grated onion
Dash of hot pepper sauce
Salt to taste
Red leaf lettuce for garnish

Cut off tops of cherry tomatoes. With a melon baller scoop out pulp and seeds. Drain tomatoes upside down on paper towels. Combine remaining ingredients and stuff tomatoes with this mixture. Arrange stuffed tomatoes in a lettuce-lined basket. Makes about 30 appetizers.

SNOW PEAS WITH SPICY SALMON FILLING

1 can (7¾ ounces) red salmon,
    drained, skin and bones removed
1 package (3 ounces) cream
    cheese, softened
2 tablespoons sour cream
1 tablespoon grated onion
1 tablespoon prepared horseradish
1 tablespoon finely chopped fresh
    dill
1 tablespoon fresh lemon juice
¼ teaspoon salt
50 snow peas, washed and strings
    removed

In a food processor puree all ingredients except pea pods; or, mince salmon, combine all ingredients in a large bowl and beat with an electric mixer until smooth. Chill salmon filling until firm, about 2 hours, before stuffing snow peas. With curved paring knife carefully slit open one side of pea pod; fill snow peas with salmon filling. Makes about 50 appetizers.

NOTE Snow peas can be stuffed up to 2 hours ahead; cover with plastic wrap and keep chilled.

STUFFED MUSHROOMS GRAZIELLA

1 large onion, minced
⅓ cup olive oil
36 medium domestic mushrooms, wiped clean and stems removed (reserve stems)
2 cups fresh bread crumbs (preferably homemade, page 126)
1 cup freshly grated Romano cheese
¼ cup currants
¼ cup pine nuts
1 tablespoon chopped fresh parsley
Salt and freshly ground black pepper to taste

In a large skillet sauté onion in olive oil until golden. With a melon baller hollow out a small indentation in each mushroom cap; set caps aside. Cut tough lower end off of reserved stems and discard. Finely chop stems and add to onions. Sauté over low heat for 3 minutes. Combine bread crumbs, cheese, currants, pine nuts, parsley and salt and pepper; stir in onion mixture. Stuff mushroom caps and place on lightly greased baking sheets. Bake in a 375°F. oven 20 to 25 minutes, or until stuffing is slightly browned. Makes 36 stuffed mushrooms.

SPINACH AND CHEVRE STUFFED MUSHROOMS

50 medium domestic mushroom caps, wiped clean and stems removed for another use
Olive oil
1 package (10 ounces) frozen spinach, thawed and well drained
½ cup Enriched Bechamel Sauce (page 123)
1 tablespoon minced green onion
¼ teaspoon freshly grated nutmeg
Salt and freshly ground black pepper to taste
6 ounces Bucheron chèvre*
6 ounces cream cheese, softened
1 tablespoon minced fresh parsley
1 tablespoon minched fresh thyme
½ teaspoon celery salt
1 clove garlic, pressed

With a melon baller hollow out a small indentation in each mushroom cap. Brush mushroom caps with oil and place on baking sheets. Combine spinach, Enriched Bechamel Sauce, onion, nutmeg, salt and pepper. Place 1 teaspoon spinach mixture in each mushroom. Combine the cheeses, parsley, thyme, celery salt and garlic. Top each mushroom with 1 teaspoon cheese mixture. Bake in a 350°F. oven about 20 minutes, or until the cheese is melted. Makes 50 stuffed mushrooms.

NOTE Any leftover spinach and cheese mixture could be used in a breakfast omelet.

*Available at better cheese shops and some gourmet markets.

FRITTATA HORS D'OEUVRES

½ of a 10-ounce package frozen chopped spinach, thawed and squeezed dry
8 ounces ricotta cheese
¾ cup freshly grated Parmesan cheese
⅔ cup chopped domestic mushrooms
2 tablespoons chopped onion
½ teaspoon crushed dried oregano leaves
1 clove garlic, pressed
1 egg
4 ounces sliced pepperoni (optional)
Sour cream for garnish (optional)

Lightly grease 24 miniature muffin cups. Mix spinach with ricotta, Parmesan, mushrooms, onion, oregano, garlic and egg. Place a slice of pepperoni in the bottom of each muffin cup, if desired. Spoon cheese mixture into cups. Bake in 375°F. oven 25 minutes, or until light golden. Cool 10 minutes, then gently loosen and remove from pans. Serve warm or cold, garnished with sour cream, if desired. Makes 24 appetizers.

NOTE For one-pan preparation, spread frittata mixture into a greased 9-inch square baking pan. Bake in a 350°F. oven 35 to 40 minutes, or until set. Cool slightly and cut into squares. Frittatas may be made ahead of time and frozen. To reheat, place in shallow pan and bake in 375°F. oven for 6 minutes.

ALMOND SHRIMP SCAMPI

2 cloves garlic, finely minced or pressed
½ cup sliced almonds
¼ pound butter
1 pound medium raw shrimp (40 to 50 per pound), peeled and deveined
½ cup minced fresh parsley
½ cup dry white wine
2 tablespoons fresh lemon juice

In a large skillet sauté garlic and almonds in butter until almonds are lightly browned, stirring occasionally. Add shrimp and cook, stirring and turning, until shrimp are opaque and cooked through, about 5 minutes. Stir in the parsley, wine and lemon juice. Serve in an attractive serving dish with toothpicks. Makes 20 appetizer servings or 3 to 4 main-course servings.

ORIENTAL CHICKEN WINGS

½ cup soy sauce
½ cup packed brown sugar
⅓ cup water
4 tablespoons butter, melted
½ teaspoon dry mustard
28 chicken wing drumettes (see Note)
Ground cinnamon
Sesame seeds

Combine soy sauce, brown sugar, water, melted butter and dry mustard. Place chicken in a single layer in a large, shallow baking pan. Pour the soy sauce mixture over the drumettes; sprinkle with cinnamon. Bake in 350°F. oven. After 30 minutes, turn the chicken with tongs, then bake 30 minutes longer; turn. Sprinkle with sesame seeds and bake an additional 30 minutes. (Total time is 1½ hours). Makes 28 appetizers.

NOTE Wing drumettes are the upper section of the chicken wing.

GOUGERE (PUFFED CHEESE RING)

1 cup milk
4 tablespoons butter
½ teaspoon salt
Dash of cayenne pepper
1 cup all-purpose flour
4 eggs, at room temperature
1 cup shredded Swiss cheese

In a 2-quart saucepan place the milk, butter, salt and cayenne. Bring to a full boil over medium heat; add flour all at once. Cook, stirring vigorously, until mixture pulls away from the sides of the pan and forms a ball, about 2 minutes. Remove from the heat; cool slightly. With a wooden spoon beat in the eggs, one at a time, mixing thoroughly after each addition. Stir in half of the cheese. Cool. On a greased cookie sheet, with an ice cream scoop or large spoon, drop 7 equal mounds of dough in a circle and touching each other (this will use about ¾ of the dough). With the remaining dough, drop a small ball on top of each large one; sprinkle with remaining cheese. Bake on the middle rack of a 375°F. oven 45 to 55 minutes, or until gougère is crisp and brown. Serve hot with butter as an appetizer or as a bread accompaniment to chicken salad or seafood salad. Makes 8 servings.

COCKTAIL PUFFS WITH THREE FILLINGS

1 recipe Pâte à Choux (Cream Puff Pastry), page 128

Prepare filling(s) of your choice. Halve puffs and fill. Arrange on baking sheets and heat in a 350°F. oven 5 minutes. Makes 24 cocktail puffs.

CREAM CHEESE FILLING

1 package (8 ounces) cream cheese, softened
¼ cup whipping cream
1 teaspoon chicken stock base
1 tablespoon finely chopped green onion, including tops
1 can (2½ ounces) chopped ripe olives, drained
1 tablespoon chopped canned green chiles

Combine cream cheese, whipping cream, chicken stock base and onion. Stir in chopped olives and green chiles. Makes 2 cups.

HAM AND PATE FILLING

1 cup cooked ground ham
1 cup liver pâté or liverwurst

Combine ham and pâté or liverwurst. Makes 2 cups.

CRAB OR SHRIMP FILLING

2 cups cooked crab meat or bay shrimp
½ cup finely chopped celery
1 hard-cooked egg, peeled and finely chopped
¼ cup mayonnaise
2 tablespoons lemon juice
1 tablespoon tomato paste
1 tablespoon minced onion
¼ teaspoon celery salt

Carefully pick over crab (if used) and remove any pieces of shell. Flake the crab meat and blend crab or shrimp with the remaining ingredients. Makes 2¾ cups.

CHICKEN LIVER AND CURRANT PATE

1 small onion, finely chopped
1 celery stalk, finely chopped
1 clove garlic, minced
½ pound butter, softened
2 pounds chicken livers, rinsed and yellow membranes removed
2 small bay leaves
4 tablespoons Calvados
¼ cup whipping cream
1 teaspoon dry mustard
¼ teaspoon salt
¼ teaspoon ground cloves
¼ teaspoon freshly grated nutmeg
½ cup currants
Assorted crackers or sliced cocktail bagels for accompaniment

In a large skillet sauté onion, celery and garlic in 6 tablespoons of the butter until tender, but not browned. Add chicken livers; cook an additional 5 minutes. Add bay leaves and Calvados. Pour into a 1½-quart ovenproof casserole, cover and bake in a 375°F. oven 20 minutes. Cool slightly; if mixture seems runny, drain off some liquid. Cool. Remove bay leaves. In a food processor puree chicken liver mixture with cream, remaining butter and seasonings. Stir in the currants; or, grind livers with a food grinder and combine with cream, remaining butter and seasonings. Turn pâté into 1-quart terrine and chill at least 4 hours, preferably overnight. Remove from refrigerator 30 minutes before serving. Serve with assorted crackers or bagels. Makes 3 cups.

CHICKEN LIVER STRUDEL

3 cups minced onions (about 2 large onions)
1 large clove garlic, pressed
6 tablespoons unsalted butter
½ pound domestic mushrooms, sliced
1 pound chicken livers, rinsed and yellow membranes removed
1 egg, lightly beaten
¼ cup dry bread crumbs (preferably homemade, page 126)
¼ cup sour cream
2 tablespoons brandy

2 tablespoons minced fresh parsley
2 tablespoons freshly grated Parmesan cheese
Salt and freshly ground black pepper to taste
8 sheets filo dough
½ pound unsalted butter, melted
½ cup dry bread crumbs (preferably homemade, page 126) combined with 2 tablespoons freshly grated Parmesan cheese
Melted butter
½ cup sour cream and 3 tablespoons minced fresh parsley for garnish

In a large skillet sauté onions and garlic in 6 tablespoons butter until golden. Stir in mushrooms and cook about 5 minutes. Increase heat slightly, add chicken livers and cook quickly until no red color appears when livers are pierced with a knife. Remove from heat. Place mixture in food processor and chop fine. Transfer to a large bowl; add egg, ¼ cup bread crumbs, sour cream, brandy, parsley, Parmesan cheese and salt and pepper. Mix thoroughly and set aside to cool.

To assemble, refer to Shaping and Forming Strudels, page 42. (Use 8 sheets filo for one large strudel and 4 each for 2 small strudels and ½ pound melted butter and bread crumb-Parmesan cheese mixture between filo layers.) Place strudel(s), seam side down, on a baking sheet; brush with melted butter. Bake in a 375°F. oven 10 minutes. Remove from oven and slice diagonally with a serrated knife about two-thirds through in the size slices desired. Brush with additional melted butter and return to oven; bake 35 to 45 minutes more, or until golden brown; cool slightly. To serve, cut through slices and garnish with sour cream and minced parsley. Makes 1 large or 2 small strudels.

FLAKY CHORIZO ROLL

1 pound ricotta cheese
1 can (4 ounces) diced green chiles
1 can (2¼ ounces) sliced ripe olives, drained
1 pound chorizo, casing removed
12 sheets filo dough
½ pound unsalted butter, melted
¾ cup dry bread crumbs (preferably homemade, page 126)
Melted butter
1 cup sour cream and 1 avocado, peeled and sliced, for garnish

In a bowl mix cheese, chiles and olives; set aside. Crumble chorizo and sauté in a medium skillet until cooked through and fat is rendered out; drain off excess fat. Set aside.

To prepare filo, refer to Shaping and Forming Strudels, page 42. (Use 6 sheets filo per strudel and melted butter and bread crumbs between filo layers.) Divide cheese mixture and chorizo into two parts, one for each strudel. Lay half the cheese mixture in a strip across the long edge of filo. Place chorizo in a strip over the cheese. Top with remaining cheese mixture. Roll up as directed. Place both rolls, seam side down, on baking sheets; brush with melted butter. Bake in a 350°F. oven 10 minutes. Remove from oven and slice strudels diagonally with a serrated knife about two-thirds through at ¾-inch intervals. Return to oven and bake 15 to 20 minutes more, or until golden brown. To serve, cut through slices. Garnish each piece with a dollop of sour cream and a slice of avocado. Makes 2 strudels (20 to 24 slices).

soups

CREAM OF RED BELL PEPPER SOUP

4 sweet red bell peppers, cored, seeded and cut in 1-inch pieces
Juice of 1 lemon, strained
4 to 5 cups Chicken Stock (page 121)
3 shallots, finely chopped
½ teaspoon salt or to taste
¼ teaspoon white pepper
3 tablespoons butter
3 tablespoons all-purpose flour
⅔ cup half-and-half
½ cup sour cream and 3 tablespoons snipped fresh chives for garnish

Combine red bell peppers and lemon juice in bowl; set aside. In a medium saucepan heat 4 cups chicken stock until simmering. Add peppers, shallots, salt and pepper. Cover and simmer 30 minutes. Transfer pepper mixture to blender using slotted spoon. Add enough of the cooking liquid to cover (reserve remaining liquid); puree. In a medium saucepan melt butter and stir in flour; cook until light golden. Add reserved cooking liquid and pureed pepper mixture; bring to a boil, reduce heat and simmer 10 minutes, stirring constantly. Remove from heat and cool slightly; add half-and-half. Thin with additional hot chicken stock, if desired. Serve hot or chilled garnished with sour cream and chives. Makes 6 to 8 servings.

NOTE This delicately colored soup was inspired by an invitational luncheon at Beringer Winery, St. Helena, California.

CREAM OF CELERY SOUP

4 cups Chicken Stock (page 121)
3 cups chopped celery, including leaves
1 cup chopped onion
1 cup milk or half-and-half
Salt and freshly ground black pepper to taste
3 tablespoons minced fresh herbs (marjoram, thyme or chervil), optional garnish

In a large soup pot combine chicken stock, celery and onion. Cook until vegetables are very tender, about 15 to 20 minutes; cool slightly. Transfer to a blender or food processor and puree. Return to soup pot, whisk in milk or half-and-half and reheat. Season with salt and pepper and garnish with minced fresh herbs, if desired. Makes 6 servings.

MUSHROOM BISQUE

½ cup finely chopped celery
3 shallots, finely chopped
4 tablespoons unsalted butter
¾ pound domestic mushrooms, sliced
1 medium potato, peeled and diced
1 cup Rich Chicken Stock (page 121)
2 teaspoons fresh thyme leaves
½ teaspoon salt or to taste
Pinch of white pepper
2 cups milk
1 cup whipping cream
¼ cup medium-dry sherry
2 tablespoons brandy
2 teaspoons soy sauce
½ cup sour cream and 3 tablespoons snipped fresh chives for garnish

In a large soup pot sauté celery and shallots in butter until translucent, about 5 minutes. Add mushrooms and cook until softened, about 5 minutes. Add diced potato, chicken stock, thyme, salt and pepper. Simmer until potatoes are very soft, about 20 minutes. In a food processor or blender puree the soup mixture, stopping occasionally to scrape down sides of the container. Return mixture to soup pot. Add milk, cream, sherry, brandy and soy sauce. Heat through, but do not boil. Serve hot, garnishing each serving with a dollop of sour cream and a sprinkling of chives. Makes 6 servings.

CREAM OF WATERCRESS SOUP

3 cups peeled and sliced Irish potatoes
3 cups thinly sliced leeks, washed thoroughly before slicing
2 quarts Chicken Stock (page 121)
Leaves and tender sprigs from 1 bunch watercress
Salt to taste
½ cup whipping cream
2 to 3 tablespoons minced fresh parsley for garnish

In a large soup pot combine the potatoes, leeks and chicken stock; bring to a boil, reduce heat and simmer 50 minutes. Remove from the heat and stir in the watercress. In a food processor or blender puree soup mixture. Season with salt, if needed. Return soup to soup pot and simmer for 5 minutes. Slowly whisk in cream. Serve in a tureen or soup bowls. Garnish with minced parsley. Makes 10 servings.

FRESH CORN AND CILANTRO SOUP

3½ cups fresh corn kernels (6 to 7 large ears of corn)
1½ cups Chicken Stock (page 121)
4 tablespoons butter
2 cups milk
1 garlic clove, pressed
1 teaspoon dried oregano leaves, crushed
Salt and freshly ground black pepper to taste
¼ cup canned diced green chiles
¼ cup chopped fresh cilantro
1 cup cubed Monterey Jack cheese
1 cup diced tomato
Tortilla chips for accompaniment

In a food processor or blender puree corn and chicken stock. In a large saucepan melt the butter over medium heat; add pureed corn and simmer 5 minutes, stirring frequently. Add milk, garlic, oregano, salt and pepper; mix well. Bring to a boil, reduce heat, then add chiles; simmer 5 minutes. Remove from heat and stir in the cilantro and cheese. Divide the diced tomatoes among 6 soup bowls. Stir soup and pour over tomatoes. Serve immediately. Makes 6 servings.

WINE COUNTRY LEMON SOUP

1 small chicken (about 2½ pounds), cut up
1 large carrot, coarsely chopped
1 stalk celery (including some leaves), coarsely chopped
1 small onion, coarsely chopped
2 bay leaves
1½ cups sauterne
Salt to taste
¼ teaspoon white pepper
½ cup raw long grain white rice
3 tablespoons butter
2 egg yolks
2 tablespoons fresh lemon juice
10 lemon slices and 3 tablespoons finely chopped fresh parsley for garnish

In a large stock pot combine chicken, carrot, celery, onion, bay leaves, 1 cup of the sauterne, salt, pepper and 2 quarts cold water. Bring to a boil, reduce heat to simmer and cook until chicken falls from the bones, about 1 hour; strain. Discard vegetables, but reserve chicken (chicken may be cut in small pieces and used in the soup or saved for another use—see Note). Chill broth until fat hardens, about 6 hours or overnight; skim. Bring broth to a boil; add rice. Cover and simmer 20 to 30 minutes, or until rice is cooked. Add butter and remaining ½ cup sauterne. Keep soup hot over low heat. In a small bowl whisk together egg yolks and lemon juice until frothy. Add 1 cup hot soup to egg yolk mixture; whisk to blend. Return this mixture to stock pot, whisking thoroughly. Heat soup, but do not boil. Serve soup immediately; garnish with lemon slices and chopped parsley. Makes 8 to 10 servings.

NOTE For a hearty luncheon soup, add 1 cup of the diced cooked chicken to the soup. When served as part of a multi-course dinner, I omit the chicken.

SPINACH AND CHEESE SOUP

6 cups Chicken Stock (page 121)
1 cup freshly grated Romano cheese
½ cup dry white wine (sauvignon blanc suggested)
2 tablespoons chopped fresh parsley
½ teaspoon salt or to taste
¼ teaspoon white pepper
1 large bunch fresh spinach, rinsed, dried, stemmed and finely shredded
6 eggs, lightly whisked

In large soup pot combine stock, cheese, wine, parsley, salt and pepper; bring to a boil. Whisk in the spinach and eggs. Reduce heat and simmer 3 minutes; adjust seasoning, if necessary. Serve immediately. Makes 6 to 8 servings.

POTAGE ST. JACQUES

4 shallots, minced
2 tablespoons butter
1 tablespoon all-purpose flour
1½ quarts Fish Stock (page 121) or clam juice (or a combination of Chicken Stock, page 121, and clam juice)
2 large or 3 medium potatoes, peeled and cut in ¼-inch slices
1 bay leaf
1 tablespoon minced fresh thyme leaves or ½ teaspoon dried thyme leaves
Salt and freshly ground black pepper to taste
1 pound scallops, coarsely chopped
2 egg yolks
1 cup half-and-half
2 tablespoons tomato paste
2 to 3 tablespoons sherry or brandy
Few drops of bitters

In a 4-quart saucepan sauté the minced shallots in butter; stir in the flour. Add the fish stock or clam juice, sliced potatoes, bay leaf, salt, pepper and thyme; cook over low heat 50 minutes. Add the scallops; simmer 5 minutes. Remove from heat; discard bay leaf. Puree in a blender or food processor. In a small bowl whisk together egg yolks and half-and-half. Add 1 cup hot soup to the egg yolk mixture; whisk to blend. Return this mixture to the soup, whisking to blend. Heat soup, but do not boil. Add tomato paste, sherry or brandy and bitters. Makes 8 servings.

NEW ENGLAND CLAM CHOWDER

6 slices bacon, diced, or 4 ounces salt pork, diced
1 medium onion, sliced
1 tablespoon all-purpose flour
½ teaspoon celery salt
¼ teaspoon white pepper
1 teaspoon fines herbes, crushed
1 bottle (8 ounces) clam juice plus drained juice from canned clams (1½ cups liquid total)
2 potatoes, peeled and diced
3 cups extra-rich milk or half-and-half
2 cans (7 ounces each) diced clams, drained and juice saved
1 tablespoon butter
1 tablespoon minced fresh parsley for garnish

In a large soup pot sauté the bacon or salt pork until lightly browned. Add the sliced onion and sauté for 2 minutes; stir in flour and seasonings and cook 1 minute. Add clam juice and potatoes. Cook, covered, over low heat until potatoes are tender, about 20 minutes. Add milk and slowly heat almost to a boil (do not boil). Stir in clams; add the butter. Stir to melt. Serve chowder with a garnish of chopped parsley. Makes 6 servings.

SPINACH AND CLAM SOUP

⅓ cup finely diced onion
2 tablespoons butter
4 anchovy fillets, minced
1 garlic clove, pressed
4 tablespoons butter
3 tablespoons all-purpose flour
4 cups Rich Chicken Stock (page 121)
1 large bunch fresh spinach, rinsed, dried, stemmed and chopped
2 cans (7 ounces each) clams, drained
1 cup whipping cream
Salt and freshly ground black pepper to taste
2 tablespoons brandy

In a medium skillet sauté onion in 2 tablespoons butter 5 minutes. Add anchovies and garlic and sauté for 1 minute. In a large saucepan cook 4 tablespoons butter and flour over medium-high heat, stirring constantly, 2 minutes. Slowly add chicken stock; bring to a boil. Add onion mixture, spinach and clams and return to a boil, stirring occasionally. Whisk in cream; bring soup almost to a boil. Season with salt and pepper. Stir in brandy. Serve immediately. Makes 6 servings.

NOTE For a smooth texture, soup may be pureed in blender just before adding cream.

DUCK LEG SOUP

8 dried shiitake mushrooms*
6 cups Duck Stock (page 122)
1 small piece daikon radish, peeled and cut in very fine julienne*
1 carrot, cut in very fine julienne
1 to 2 cups slivered duck leg meat
1 to 2 teaspoons sesame oil
1½ cups shredded Napa cabbage
Salt to taste
1 to 2 teaspoons mushroom soy sauce (optional, see Note)
½ cup fresh cilantro leaves for garnish

Soak shiitake mushrooms in warm water to cover until softened, about 30 minutes; drain and squeeze out excess moisture. Cut into ¼-inch strips; set aside. Heat duck stock. (For a richer tasting soup, reduce stock over high heat to 5 cups.) Add daikon, carrot, slivered duck leg meat, mushroom strips and sesame oil to stock; cook 5 minutes. Remove from heat. Stir in shredded cabbage. Season with salt, if needed. Served garnished with cilantro. Makes 6 servings.

NOTE If a richer brown color is desired, add 1 to 2 teaspoons mushroom soy sauce, available at oriental markets. Additional salt may not be needed if soy is added.

*Available at oriental and specialty produce markets.

TORTILLA SOUP

3 quarts Chicken Stock (page 121)
8 tomatoes, peeled, seeded and
   cut in large dice
2 green bell peppers, cored,
   seeded and cut in 1-inch cubes
1 large onion, diced
½ cup chopped fresh cilantro
   leaves
1 clove garlic, minced
½ teaspoon ground cumin
¼ teaspoon crushed red pepper
   flakes
⅛ teaspoon white pepper
1⅓ cups corn kernels (2 large ears
   of corn)
4 green onions, minced
1 zucchini, sliced in ¼-inch rounds
1½ cups shredded cooked chicken
1 cup cooked rice
Salt
Tortilla chips, and 1 cup shredded
   Monterey Jack or Cheddar
   cheese for accompaniment

In a large soup pot combine stock, tomatoes, green peppers, onion, cilantro, garlic, cumin, red pepper flakes and white pepper; bring to a boil. Reduce heat, cover and simmer 30 minutes. Add corn and green onions; cook 10 minutes. Stir in zucchini, chicken and rice. Cook just until zucchini is tender, about 6 minutes. Season with salt, if needed. To serve, ladle into individual bowls. Top with tortilla chips and cheese. Serve immediately so chips do not become soggy. Makes 10 servings.

ITALIAN GUMBO

1½ pounds mild Italian sausage,
   cut in ¼-inch slices
2 tablespoons safflower oil
3 cloves garlic, pressed
½ cup diced onion
6 large tomatoes, peeled, seeded
   and cut in 1-inch chunks
5 cups Beef Stock (page 122)
1½ cups dry red wine
½ teaspoon dried oregano,
   crushed
¼ cup chopped fresh parsley
1 large green bell pepper, cored,
   seeded and diced
2 medium zucchini, cut in ¼-inch
   rounds
1½ cups small fusilli or miniature
   bow knot pasta
1 tablespoon minced fresh basil
1 can (8 ounces) clams, including
   liquid (optional)
⅔ cup freshly grated Parmesan
   cheese for garnish

In a heavy-bottomed soup pot cook the sausage over medium heat until lightly browned, about 8 minutes. Remove the sausage with a slotted spoon and drain on paper toweling. Pour off all fat. Sauté the garlic and onion in the safflower oil. Add the sausage, tomatoes, stock, wine, and oregano and simmer 30 minutes. Add the parsley, green pepper, zucchini and pasta; simmer 15 minutes, or until pasta is al dente. Stir in fresh basil. Add clams, if desired, and heat through. Ladle into soup tureen or soup bowls and sprinkle with Parmesan cheese. Makes 8 to 10 servings.

AVOCADO GAZPACHO

1 quart tomato juice
½ cup tomato puree
3 medium avocados, peeled and
    cubed
1 medium cucumber, peeled and
    chopped (about 1 cup)
1 large green pepper, cored,
    seeded and chopped (about 1
    cup)
2 large tomatoes, chopped
½ cup green onion, finely chopped
2 tablespoons minced fresh parsley
1 clove garlic, pressed
2 tablespoons fresh lemon or lime
    juice
½ teaspoon hot pepper sauce
½ teaspoon salt
⅛ teaspoon white pepper
¾ cup croutons for garnish

In a large bowl combine all ingredients except croutons; chill thoroughly, 2 to 3 hours. Serve in
chilled bowls. Garnish with croutons. Makes 6 servings.

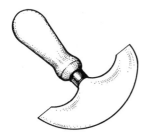

MELON SOUP WITH STRAWBERRIES

1 pint strawberries, washed and
    hulled
4 medium ripe cantaloupes, rind
    and seeds removed
2 cups Muscat Canelli wine or
    sweet Riesling wine
1 cup fresh orange juice
1 cup pineapple juice or papaya
    nectar
⅓ cup fresh lime juice
1 bottle champagne or 1 bottle car-
    bonated lemon-lime beverage

Halve large strawberries; chill. With
melon baller cut balls from one of
the cantaloupes; chill melon balls.
Cut remaining 3 melons into
chunks. Place chunks and any cantaloupe remaining from making
balls in a food processor. Process
until smooth; or, puree in a blender
in 3 small batches (some pineapple
juice may need to be added with
each batch). In a chilled soup tureen place cantaloupe puree, wine
orange, pineapple, and lime juices.
(The soup may be made ahead of
time to this point and refrigerated.)
To serve, pour in champagne or
lemon-lime beverage; stir. Add
strawberries and melon balls.
Makes 10 to 12 servings.

LINGONBERRY CHERRY SOUP

3 tablespoons quick-cooking
    tapioca
½ cup sugar
¼ teaspoon salt
2 sticks cinnamon
Zest of 1 lemon, cut fine
1½ cups frozen tart cherries
1 jar (8 ounces) lingonberries*
⅓ cup fresh lemon juice
½ cup sour cream for garnish

In an acid-resistant saucepan combine 2 cups water, tapioca, sugar,
salt, cinnamon, lemon zest and
cherries. Bring mixture to a boil
over medium-high heat, stirring
constantly. Reduce heat and simmer, stirring, 5 minutes. Remove
from heat and remove cinnamon
stick; stir in lingonberries and
lemon juice. Ladle soup into bowls.
Garnish each with a dollop of sour
cream. Makes 6 servings.

*Lingonberries are usually found in
gourmet markets or well-stocked
supermarkets. If unavailable, omit
and increase sugar by 2 tablespoons.

salads

THREE MUSHROOM AND PINE NUT SALAD WITH BALSAMIC VINAIGRETTE

1 bunch watercress, washed
1 head Belgian endive, washed and
    cut crosswise in small pieces
2 heads red leaf or butter lettuce or
    1 of each, washed, leaves sepa-
    rated and torn in bite-sized
    pieces
2 to 3 tablespoons chopped fresh
    herbs (basil, chervil or tarragon)
1 pound oyster mushrooms*
4 ounces chanterelle mushrooms,
    cut in bite-sized pieces*
¼ cup walnut oil (or combination of
    walnut oil and olive oil)
½ cup toasted pine nuts (page 126)
Balsamic Vinaigrette (following)
1 package enoki mushrooms, for
    garnish*

Combine all prepared greens and herbs in large salad bowl. In a large, heavy bottomed skillet sauté oyster and chanterelle mushrooms in ¼ cup walnut oil until golden. Stir in toasted pine nuts. Add sautéed mushrooms and pine nuts to the mixed greens. Toss with Balsamic Vinaigrette. Garnish with enoki mushrooms. Makes 6 servings.

BALSAMIC VINAIGRETTE In a small bowl whisk together ⅓ cup walnut oil, ¼ cup balsamic vinegar and salt and freshly ground black pepper to taste.

NOTE This salad may also be served on individual plates as an appetizer course. The top may be garnished with baby shrimp, fingers of crab or slices of smoked duck.

*Available at oriental or specialty produce markets.

GARDEN FRESH SALAD WITH TARRAGON VINAIGRETTE

1 head butter lettuce, leaves sepa-
    rated and torn in bite-sized
    pieces
1 head Belgian endive, leaves sep-
    arated and cut in crosswise
    slices
1 head radicchio, torn in bite-sized
    pieces (optional)
4 ounces cooked bay shrimp
3 ounces Roquefort cheese,
    crumbled
1 package enoki mushrooms*
½ cup toasted walnuts (page 126)
Tarragon Vinaigrette (following)

Combine salad greens in an attractive salad bowl. Decoratively arrange the shrimp, cheese, mushrooms and toasted walnuts on the top of the mixed greens; chill. When ready to serve, pour dressing over the salad and toss to mix. Makes 6 servings.

TARRAGON VINAIGRETTE In a small bowl whisk together 1 egg yolk and 1 teaspoon Dijon-style mustard. Add ¼ cup tarragon vinegar, then slowly whisk in ⅔ cup olive oil (or combination of olive and walnut oils). Season with 2 tablespoons minced fresh tarragon and salt and freshly ground black pepper to taste.

*Available at oriental or specialty produce markets.

GREEN BEAN AND WALNUT SALAD

1 tablespoon salt
2 pounds fresh green beans, trimmed and cut diagonally in bite-sized pieces
1 cup toasted walnuts, chopped (page 126)
1 cup diced red onion
1 cup crumbled Bulgarian feta cheese
Walnut-Mint Dressing (following)

In a large saucepan bring 6 quarts water to a boil. Add 1 tablespoon salt and the beans and cook until crisp-tender, about 5 to 7 minutes. Drain well. Plunge beans into ice water to stop the cooking process; drain and pat dry. Arrange beans in glass serving bowl. Top with nuts, onion and cheese. Just before serving, pour dressing over salad and toss to mix. Makes 6 to 8 servings.

WALNUT-MINT DRESSING In a medium bowl whisk together ½ cup olive oil, ¼ cup walnut oil, 6 tablespoons white wine vinegar, ½ cup finely chopped fresh mint leaves, 2 pressed garlic cloves, ½ teaspoon salt and ¼ teaspoon freshly ground black pepper.

FRESH GREEN BEAN AND TOMATO SALAD

1 tablespoon salt
1 pound fresh green beans, trimmed and cut diagonally in bite-sized pieces
4 tomatoes, peeled and quartered
4 ounces feta cheese, crumbled (optional)
Herb Vinaigrette (following)

In large saucepan bring 6 quarts water to a boil. Add 1 tablespoon salt and the beans and cook until crisp-tender, about 5 to 7 minutes. Drain well. Plunge beans into ice water to stop the cooking process; drain and pat dry. Combine green beans, tomatoes and feta cheese, if desired, in a serving bowl. Pour dressing over salad and chill. Makes 6 servings.

HERB VINAIGRETTE In a small bowl whisk together 3 tablespoons olive oil, 1 tablespoon wine vinegar, 1 pressed garlic clove, 1 teaspoon chopped fresh dill or ½ teaspoon dried dill weed, 1 teaspoon minced fresh parsley, ¼ teaspoon Dijon-style mustard and salt and freshly ground black pepper to taste.

SPINACH CRUNCH SALAD

2 bunches fresh spinach (6 cups), rinsed, dried, stemmed and torn in bite-sized pieces
8 ounces Longhorn Cheddar cheese, cut in thin strips
3 hard-cooked eggs, peeled and chopped
⅓ cup chopped salted peanuts
⅓ cup unsweetened shredded coconut
¼ cup sliced green onions (including some of the green tops)
Zesty Dressing (following)

In a large bowl toss together spinach, cheese, eggs, peanuts, coconut and green onions. Pour dressing over salad and toss. Makes 8 servings.

ZESTY DRESSING In a medium bowl whisk together 1 cup sour cream, ½ cup mayonnaise, 1 tablespoon sugar, 1 tablespoon white wine vinegar, 1 tablespoon prepared horseradish, 1 teaspoon prepared mustard, ½ teaspoon salt and 1 minced garlic clove; chill.

ITALIAN CARROT AND CAULIFLOWER SALAD

2 cups sliced carrots, cooked crisp-tender
2 cups cauliflowerets, cooked crisp-tender
1 cup celery cut in ¼-inch pieces
1 sweet red bell pepper, cored, seeded and cut in julienne
3 cloves garlic, minced
2 small dried hot red chiles
1 bay leaf
⅔ cup imported white wine vinegar
⅔ cup virgin olive oil
½ cup Kalamata olives*
2 tablespoons drained capers

Combine carrots, cauliflowerets, celery and red bell pepper in salad bowl. In a small saucepan combine garlic, chiles, bay leaf and vinegar. Bring to a boil, reduce heat and simmer 3 minutes. Pour hot vinegar mixture over combined vegetables. Stir in the olive oil, olives and capers; toss. Chill at least 6 hours, preferably overnight. Serve at room temperature. Makes 6 to 8 servings.

*Available at Italian or Greek delicatessens.

SAFFRON ZUCCHINI SALAD

5 tablespoons olive oil
4 small zucchini, thinly sliced
1 sweet red bell pepper, cored, seeded and cut in ¼-inch strips
3 shallots, finely chopped
Pinch of saffron infused in 2 tablespoons water
2 teaspoons snipped fresh dill
1 teaspoon sugar
Salt and freshly ground black pepper to taste
5 tablespoons white wine vinegar

In a large skillet heat olive oil over medium heat. Add zucchini, red bell pepper and shallots and cook 5 minutes, stirring occasionally (do not allow to brown). Add the dissolved saffron-water mixture, dill, sugar, salt, pepper and vinegar. Continue cooking until zucchini is just tender, about 5 minutes. Transfer to salad bowl and cool. Cover and chill. Serve chilled or at room temperature. Makes 6 servings.

NOTE The flavor of this salad is reminiscent of the Mediterranean and it goes nicely with foods of that region.

ZUCCHINI SALAD A LA GRECQUE

2 medium zucchini cut into 1-inch
   fine julienne
1 small green bell pepper, cored,
   seeded and diced
2 small tomatoes, coarsely
   chopped
4 ounces Monterey Jack cheese,
   cut in fine julienne
¼ cup fresh parsley leaves, minced
10 Greek olives, halved and pitted*
Anchovy Dressing (following)

Place the vegetables, cheese, parsley and olives in serving bowl. Pour dressing over and toss. Chill until ready to serve. Makes 6 to 8 servings.

ANCHOVY DRESSING In a small bowl whisk together ¼ cup fresh lemon juice, 2 tablespoons olive oil, 2 tablespoons vegetable oil, 1 tablespoon wine vinegar, 1 tablespoon anchovy paste, 2 teaspoons snipped fresh dill and a pinch of dried, crumbled oregano leaves.

NOTE The salad may also be served in halves of fresh pita bread.

*Available at Italian and Greek delicatessens.

CRUNCHY COLESLAW

½ cup bulgur wheat
¼ teaspoon salt
½ cup mayonnaise
3 tablespoons white wine vinegar
¼ teaspoon liquid hot pepper
   sauce
2 tablespoons sugar
1 teaspoon snipped fresh dill
¼ teaspoon Dijon-style mustard
½ cup thinly sliced green onion
2½ cups finely shredded cabbage
½ cup thinly sliced celery
½ cup shredded carrot
Salt and freshly ground black pepper to taste

In a medium saucepan combine the bulgur, 1 cup water and salt; bring to a boil, stir, and simmer, covered, 15 minutes, or until liquid is absorbed. Meanwhile whisk together the mayonnaise, vinegar, hot pepper sauce, sugar, dill, mustard and green onion. Stir dressing into cooked wheat; chill thoroughly. About 1 hour before serving, combine the cabbage, celery and carrot and stir in the wheat mixture. Season with salt and pepper, if necessary. Spoon the mixture into a salad bowl and chill until serving time. Makes 6 servings.

CALIFORNIA RANCH COLESLAW

2 carrots, cut in fine julienne
2 zucchini, cut in fine julienne
1 green bell pepper, cored, seeded
   and cut in fine julienne
2 celery stalks, cut in fine julienne
½ head white cabbage, shredded
½ head red cabbage, shredded
Ranch Dressing (following)
2 tablespoons minced fresh parsley
   for garnish

Combine the vegetables in a large bowl and toss. Pour dressing over vegetables and toss. Just before serving, sprinkle the salad with the minced parsley. Makes 6 servings.

RANCH DRESSING In a small bowl whisk together ⅔ cup olive oil, ¼ cup fresh lemon juice, 2 egg yolks, 1 teaspoon Dijon-style mustard and salt and freshly ground black pepper to taste.

ELEPHANT GARLIC SALAD

2 cloves elephant garlic*
1 large green bell pepper
1 large sweet red bell pepper
1 large yellow bell pepper
1 head curly endive or red leaf lettuce, leaves separated and torn in bite-sized pieces
4 ounces Montrachet or Bucheron chèvre*
Raspberry-Walnut Vinaigrette (following)

In a small saucepan poach un-peeled elephant garlic cloves 10 minutes in 1 cup water; drain and cool. While garlic is cooling, prepare the salad. Roast peppers (page 126) and cut in ¼-inch strips. Arrange endive or red leaf lettuce on 6 salad plates. Slice cheese into small pieces and sprinkle over the greens. Arrange the roasted pepper strips over the greens. Peel and thinly slice the poached garlic cloves and arrange on the top of the salad. Pour dressing over salad. Makes 6 servings.

RASPBERRY-WALNUT
VINAIGRETTE In a medium bowl whisk together ¼ cup olive oil, ¼ cup walnut oil, ¼ cup raspberry vinegar, ¼ teaspoon salt and ¼ teaspoon freshly ground black pepper.

*Elephant garlic is a head of garlic about the size of an apple and is milder in flavor than regular garlic. It is generally available at specialty produce markets and some Italian delicatessens. If unavailable, substitute 8 cloves regular garlic.

Chèvre is available at better cheese shops and some gourmet markets.

INDONESIAN VEGETABLE SALAD

½ head lettuce, shredded
2 cups shredded Napa cabbage, blanched for 1 minute and well drained
6 carrots, cut in ¼-inch by 2-inch sticks and cooked crisp-tender
1 pound green beans, cut on the diagonal in 2-inch pieces and cooked crisp-tender
1 medium daikon radish,* peeled and cut in 2-inch julienne, or 1 cup julienne jícama
1 hothouse cucumber, scored with mushroom fluter or fork and sliced in ¼-inch rounds
2 hard-cooked eggs, peeled and quartered
3 tomatoes, quartered
Peanut Sauce (following)

In center of large serving dish arrange the lettuce in a mound. Spread the cabbage over the top of the lettuce. Arrange the carrots and green beans neatly around the lettuce and cabbage. Arrange the daikon or jícama, cucumber and eggs in an attractive pattern around the outer edge of the salad. Place the tomato quarters across the top of the mounded lettuce and cabbage. Serve with Peanut Sauce. Makes 6 to 8 servings.

PEANUT SAUCE In a small saucepan bring ½ cup thawed frozen unsweetened coconut milk and ¼ cup water to a simmer. Remove from heat and whisk in ½ cup creamy peanut butter. Add 2 tablespoons Shaosing wine* or dry sherry, 2 tablespoons fresh lemon juice, 1 tablespoon packed brown sugar, ½ to 1 teaspoon chili paste* and ¼ teaspoon salt and whisk until smooth. Add 2 tablespoons minced fresh cilantro, if desired. Cool sauce, but do not refrigerate. If sauce is too thick (it should be the consistency of a heavy salad dressing) thin with warm water.

*Available at oriental markets.

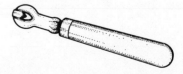

KIWI, KUMQUAT AND JICAMA SALAD WITH AVOCADO-LIME DRESSING

1 head red leaf lettuce and 1 head
    butter lettuce, washed and torn in
    pieces
4 kiwifruit, peeled and sliced
16 fresh kumquats, quartered and
    seeds removed (see Note)
¾ cup jícama strips
Avocado-Lime Dressing (following)
¼ cup pomegranate seeds (op-
    tional in season) for garnish

In large salad bowl, combine let-
tuces, kiwi, kumquats and jícama.
Pour dressing over salad and toss.
Garnish with pomegranate seeds, if
available. Serve immediately.
Makes 6 servings.

AVOCADO-LIME DRESSING In a
food processor or blender puree 2
ripe avocados, peeled and cut into
large chunks; ½ cup sour cream; 5
tablespoons fresh lime juice; 1 tablespoon grated onion; 1 teaspoon
prepared horseradish; 1 teaspoon
sugar; 1 teaspoon grated orange
peel and a few drops hot pepper
sauce; or, mash avocados with a
potato masher and combine with
remaining ingredients.

NOTE An 8-ounce can mandarin
oranges, drained, may be substituted for the kumquats when they
are not in season.

ORANGE AND ALMOND TOSSED GREEN SALAD

6 cups torn mixed greens (red leaf,
    butter and romaine lettuce)
3 oranges, peeled and sectioned
1 cup thinly sliced celery
¼ cup sliced green onions
½ cup toasted slivered almonds
    (page 126)
Almond Dressing (following)

In a large salad bowl combine
greens, oranges, celery and green
onions; sprinkle with almonds. Pour
dressing over salad and toss gently.
Serve at once. Makes 8 servings.

ALMOND DRESSING In a small bowl
whisk together ⅓ cup vegetable oil,
3 tablespoons white wine vinegar, 2
tablespoons sugar, salt and ⅛ teaspoon almond extract; chill.

GRAPEFRUIT, PAPAYA, AVOCADO AND WATERCRESS SALAD

2 bunches watercress, washed and
    trimmed for tender sprigs
3 grapefruit, peeled and sectioned
1 papaya, peeled and sliced in ½-
    inch slices
1 avocado, peeled and sliced
Tart French Dressing (page 124)

On each of 6 salad plates, arrange
a bed of watercress sprigs. Arrange
the slices of grapefruit, papaya and
avocado in a pinwheel on the watercress. Serve well chilled with Tart
French Dressing. Makes 6 servings.

NOTE This colorful and light salad
fits nicely between the main course
and dessert at a dinner party.

PEAR WALDORF SALAD

3 winter pears, cored and diced
2 tablespoons fresh lemon juice
¾ cup diced Swiss cheese
½ cup diced celery
½ cup chopped walnuts
⅔ cup mayonnaise
Lettuce leaves for garnish

In a large bowl combine the pears
and lemon juice. Stir in the Swiss
cheese, celery and chopped walnuts, then the mayonnaise. Chill
and serve on lettuce leaves. Makes
6 to 8 servings.

MINTY ORANGE, ONION AND CUCUMBER SALAD

2 hothouse cucumbers or 3 regular
   cucumbers, peeled and halved
   lengthwise
2 navel oranges, peeled and sectioned, or 1 can (11 ounces)
   mandarin orange segments,
   drained
1 small red onion, cut in thin rings
½ cup chopped fresh mint leaves
¼ cup minced fresh parsley
Zest from 1 orange (removed with
   zester and cut in ½-inch lengths)
Walnut Dressing (following)

With melon baller scoop out seeds
the length of each cucumber. Cut
cucumber halves crosswise into ¼-
inch crescents. Combine cucumber
crescents, orange sections, onion
rings, mint, parsley and orange
zest. Pour dressing over salad, toss
to combine and refrigerate for several hours to allow flavors to blend.
Toss again just prior to serving.
Makes 6 servings.

WALNUT DRESSING In a small bowl
whisk together ¼ cup walnut oil, ¼
cup virgin olive oil, ½ cup raspberry
wine vinegar or red wine vinegar
and 2 tablespoons sugar.

NOTE This salad goes well with
roast or barbecued lamb and would
also be nice for a Middle Eastern
buffet.

STRAWBERRY-SPINACH SALAD

1 bunch fresh spinach, rinsed,
   dried, stemmed and torn in bite-
   sized pieces
1 cup jícama strips
1 pint strawberries, washed and
   hulled
1 to 2 cups bean sprouts
Strawberry Vinaigrette (following)

In a salad bowl toss together spinach, jícama strips, strawberries and
bean sprouts. Pour dressing over
salad and serve. Makes 6 servings.

STRAWBERRY VINAIGRETTE In a
medium bowl whisk together 1 cup
pureed strawberries (1 pint whole
berries), ¼ cup vegetable oil, 2 tablespoons sugar, ½ teaspoon sesame oil and salt and freshly ground
black pepper to taste.

AVOCADO SHELLS FILLED WITH CARROT AND ORANGE SALAD

¼ cup raisins
1 cup orange juice
½ teaspoon finely grated fresh ginger root
⅛ teaspoon crushed red pepper
   flakes
3 cups coarsely grated carrots (7 to
   8 medium carrots)
3 large ripe avocados
¼ cup fresh lemon juice
6 butter lettuce leaves for garnish

Plump raisins by soaking in hot
water for 20 minutes; drain. Combine orange juice, ginger and red
pepper flakes. Place carrots and
raisins in large bowl and pour orange juice marinade over. Marinate
2 hours; drain and reserve marinade. Just before serving prepare
avocado shells. Cut avocados in
half, remove pits and peel. Sprinkle
avocados with lemon juice. Line 6
salad plates with the butter lettuce
leaves. Place an avocado half on
each leaf. Divide the carrot salad
among the avocado halves. Spoon
some of the orange juice marinade
over the top of each salad. Makes 6
servings.

CARVED WATERMELON BASKET WITH FRESH FRUITS

1 large watermelon
1 honeydew melon, halved and seeded
1 cantaloupe, peeled, halved lengthwise and seeded
4 kiwifruit, peeled and cut in thin slices
1 pint strawberries, washed and hulled
½ cup Mint Syrup (following), optional

Remove two sections of watermelon from upper portion, leaving a rounded piece to form the handle (page 32). With melon baller, scoop and cut melon balls. Remove any remaining red watermelon flesh from inside melon. With melon "v" tool cut notches around edge of watermelon basket. With melon baller scoop and cut honeydew melon balls. For variety cut cantaloupe with crinkle cutter into small wavy chunks. Combine the melon balls and chunks with the kiwi and strawberries. Place fruit in watermelon basket and pour Mint Syrup over fruit. Chill until serving time. Makes 12 servings.

MINT SYRUP In a small saucepan combine ½ cup sugar and ½ cup water. Bring to a boil and boil 2 minutes; cool slightly. Pour over ½ cup fresh mint leaves. Cool syrup and strain.

ORANGES, KIWI AND PINEAPPLE WITH ROSE WATER SYRUP

½ cup sugar
3 tablespoons rose water*
3 oranges, peeled and sectioned
3 kiwifruit, peeled and sliced
½ fresh pineapple, cut into chunks
1 cup blueberries, fresh or frozen (see Note)

In a small saucepan bring sugar and 1 cup water to a boil; cook 5 minutes. Remove from heat and cool to room temperature. Stir in the rose water; chill. Combine prepared fruits in a serving bowl. Pour syrup over the fruits. Makes 8 servings.

NOTE If frozen blueberries are used, add them to the chilled fruit just before serving.

*Available at drugstores, specialty food stores and Middle Eastern markets.

COUNTRY INN SALAD

2 cups Trail Mix (following)
3 large navel oranges, peeled and sectioned
3 bananas, peeled and sliced in ¼-inch rounds
3 large firm pears, quartered, cored and sliced
2 pink grapefruits, peeled and sectioned
Creamy Maple Dressing (following)

Combine the trail mix and prepared fruits in a large bowl. Pour dressing over the fruits and toss lightly; cover and chill. Toss again just before serving.

TRAIL MIX Combine ½ cup unsweetened coconut chips, ½ cup raisins, ½ cup unsalted sunflower seeds, ½ cup unsalted dry roasted peanuts, ¼ cup pepitas (optional) and ¼ cup chopped or thinly sliced dried apricots, papaya or pineapple (optional).

CREAMY MAPLE DRESSING In a small bowl whisk together 1 cup sour cream, 1 cup plain yogurt, 3 tablespoons pure maple syrup and ½ teaspoon ground cinnamon.

light entrees

EGGPLANT, ITALIAN SAUSAGE AND DRIED TOMATO PIZZA

1 recipe Basic Pizza Dough (page 130)
1 medium onion, chopped
2 tablespoons olive oil
1 large clove garlic, pressed
1 can (15 ounces) tomato sauce
2 tablespoons chopped fresh basil
1 teaspoon dried oregano leaves, crushed
3 links mild Italian sausage, casings removed
Vegetable oil
2 Japanese eggplants, peeled and cut in julienne
⅓ cup chopped drained Dried Tomatoes (page 46)
¾ cup grated mozzarella cheese
¾ cup grated Italian Fontina cheese

Prepare pizza dough; set aside to rise. In a large skillet sauté the onion in olive oil over medium heat until limp. Stir in garlic, tomato sauce, basil and oregano; bring to a boil, reduce heat, and simmer uncovered, until very thick, 12 to 15 minutes, stirring several times. Set aside to cool.

In a medium skillet crumble sausage and fry until cooked through. Drain and pat with a paper towel to remove excess grease. In the same skillet stir fry the eggplant in a small amount of oil until crisp-tender.

Shape pizza dough according to Basic Pizza Dough recipe. Spread sauce over dough, then top with sausage, eggplant and dried tomatoes. Sprinkle with cheeses. For pizza pan: Bake on lowest rack of preheated 425°F. oven 15 to 20 minutes, or until crust is golden brown. For baking stone: Preheat stone in 425°F. 30 minutes while shaping pizza. Slip prepared pizza from baker's peel onto baking stone. Bake 15 to 20 minutes, or until crust is golden brown. Cut with pizza cutter and serve immediately. Makes one 14-inch pizza.

RED PEPPER, ARTICHOKE AND PROSCIUTTO VARIATION Substitute 1 cored, seeded and julienned large sweet red bell pepper; 1 cooked, drained and cut-up 9-ounce package frozen artichoke hearts; and 4 ounces julienned prosciutto for the eggplant, sausage and dried tomatoes.

SHRIMP, RED ONION AND CHEVRE PIZZA

1 recipe Basic Pizza Dough (page
    130)
1⅓ cups sliced red onion
2 tablespoons butter
2 tablespoons olive oil
Salt and freshly ground black pep-
    per to taste
⅓ pound medium raw shrimp,
    shelled, deveined and halved
    lengthwise
2 tablespoons olive oil
1 clove garlic, minced
Rosemary flavored olive oil (from
    dried tomatoes)
4 ounces Bucheron chèvre, diced*
⅓ cup Italian Fontina cheese
⅓ cup sliced drained Dried Toma-
    toes (page 46)
2 tablespoons freshly grated Par-
    mesan or Romano cheese

Prepare pizza dough; set aside to
rise. In large skillet sauté red onion
in butter and olive oil over medium-
low heat 5 minutes; reduce heat to
low, cover and cook until tender, 15
to 20 minutes. Season lightly with
salt and pepper; cool. In a small
bowl combine shrimp, 2 tablespoons olive oil and garlic and set
aside to marinate.

Shape pizza dough according to
Basic Pizza Dough recipe. Brush
dough with rosemary-flavored olive
oil. Combine chèvre and Fontina
cheeses and sprinkle half of
cheese mixture over pizza. Top with
red onion, then tomatoes. Sprinkle
remaining cheese mixture over
pizza. For pizza pan: Bake on lowest rack of 425°F. oven 15 to 20
minutes, or until crust is golden
brown. For baking stone: Preheat
stone in 425°F. oven 30 minutes
while shaping pizza. Slip prepared
pizza from baker's peel onto baking
stone. Bake 20 to 25 minutes, or
until crust is golden brown. Drain
shrimp and arrange on top of pizza
and continue baking until shrimp
turn pink, about 2 to 3 minutes. Remove pizza from oven and brush
edges with olive oil. Sprinkle with
Parmesan or Romano cheese. Cut
with pizza cutter and serve immediately. Makes one 14-inch pizza.

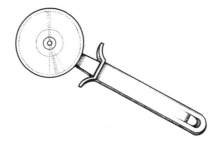

SALMON AND FRESH ASPARAGUS PASTA

1 pint whipping cream
2 tablespoons unsalted butter
½ teaspoon salt
Few gratings of fresh nutmeg
1½ cups flaked poached salmon
    (page 94)
3 tablespoons freshly grated Parmi-
    giano-Reggiano cheese
¼ cup snipped fresh dill
1 cup fresh asparagus pieces, cut
    in 1-inch lengths and cooked
    crisp-tender
1 pound Spinach Pasta (page 131),
    or 12 ounces dried pasta
6 small sprigs of fresh dill for
    garnish

In a large saucepan combine the
cream and butter and bring to a
simmer. Add salt and nutmeg and
simmer until cream is reduced by
one-third. Add salmon, Parmesan
cheese, dill and asparagus; heat
through. Meanwhile, cook the pasta
in rapidly boiling salted water until
al dente, 2 to 3 minutes for fresh
pasta or 8 to 10 minutes for dried
pasta; drain. Toss sauce with
cooked pasta. Divide among 6
small plates. Garnish with fresh dill
sprigs. Makes 6 first-course servings.

NOTE This pasta has a light, delicate flavor and can be served for
brunch.

FETTUCCINE WITH SHRIMP, SCALLOP AND CLAM SAUCE

⅓ cup minced green onion (use white part only)
¼ cup olive oil
3 tablespoons butter
2 cloves garlic, minced or pressed
½ pound medium raw shrimp, peeled and deveined
½ pound bay scallops
1 can (7½ ounces) chopped clams, drained
⅔ cup dry white wine
1 cup canned peeled plum tomatoes in extra puree
2 tablespoons minced fresh basil
2 tablespoons chopped fresh Italian parsley
2 tablespoons brandy
Pinch of dried oregano
Pinch of crushed hot red pepper flakes
1 pound Basic Pasta (page 130) or 12 ounces dried pasta
1 teaspoon olive oil

In a large skillet sauté the green onion in olive oil and butter over medium heat for 2 minutes. Add garlic and sauté 1 minute. Add the shrimp and sauté until they start to turn pink. Add the scallops and sauté 2 minutes. Stir in the chopped clams and wine; simmer 3 minutes. Add the tomatoes, basil, parsley, brandy, oregano and pepper flakes. Simmer, covered, 3 to 5 minutes. Meanwhile, cook the pasta in rapidly boiling, salted water until al dente, 2 to 3 minutes for fresh pasta, or 8 to 10 minutes for dried pasta; drain. Add 1 teaspoon olive oil to cooked pasta and toss. Place pasta on warm platter and top with sauce. Makes 4 servings.

FRESH PASTA IN A SAUCE OF SAUTEED SCALLOPS AND SNOW PEAS WITH CASCABEL CHILES

4 dried cascabel chiles*
⅔ cup whipping cream
3 tablespoons dry vermouth
3 large shallots, minced
3 tablespoons butter
8 green onions (including green tops), cut in ¾-inch diagonal pieces
1½ pounds scallops, quartered, or 1½ pounds bay scallops
2 teaspoons fresh lime juice
20 snow peas, strings removed and cut in ¾-inch lengths
Salt and freshly ground black pepper to taste
1 pound Red Bell Pepper Pasta (page 131)

In a small saucepan boil chiles in 2 cups water for five minutes. Remove from heat and cool. Drain chiles; stem, seed and devein. In a food processor or blender combine chiles, cream and vermouth and process just until chiles are ground (don't whip cream too long or it will become stiff); set aside. In a large skillet sauté shallots in butter over medium-high heat until translucent. Stir in green onions and sauté 1 minute. Add scallops and cook until scallops are barely firm, about 3 to 5 minutes. Sprinkle with lime juice. With a slotted spoon, remove scallops and onions from skillet. Pour chile puree into skillet and bring to boil. Cook until reduced by one-third. Return scallop and onion mixture to sauce; add snow peas and cook 1 minute. Taste and season with salt and pepper, if needed. Meanwhile, cook pasta in rapidly boiling, salted water until al dente, about 2 to 3 minutes; drain. Spoon sauce over pasta and serve. Makes 6 first-course servings.

*Available at Latin American markets.

Photograph: Red Bell Pepper, Artichoke and Prosciutto Pizza.

SCALLOP RAVIOLI WITH TARRAGON-SAFFRON SAUCE

½ pound scallops, rinsed and drained
1 egg white
⅓ cup whipping cream
1 tablespoon snipped fresh chives
Salt and white pepper to taste
1 pound Basic Pasta Dough (page 130)
2 tablespoons minced shallots
1 tablespoon butter
1¼ cups Chicken Stock (page 121)
¾ cup dry white wine
1 to 2 tablespoons finely chopped fresh tarragon
Small pinch saffron infused in 2 tablespoons chicken stock
½ cup whipping cream
¼ pound butter
Salt to taste

In a food processor or blender puree scallops, egg white, cream, chives, salt and pepper. Chill, covered, for several hours. Roll pasta dough through #5 setting on the hand pasta machine. Lay flat sheets of pasta out on board. Place

Photograph: Pasta and Seafood Salad Provençal, served in tomato basket.

filling on pasta at 3-inch intervals. Cover with second sheet of pasta. Cut and crimp pasta with the pastry crimper or ravioli cutter into 3-inch squares. Bring 4 to 5 quarts water to boil. Add 1 tablespoon salt and ravioli; cook 5 to 7 minutes. To test for doneness, after 5 minutes cut one ravioli in half to be sure filling is cooked. In a large, heavy-bottomed saucepan sauté shallots in 1 tablespoon butter. Add chicken stock, wine, tarragon and saffron; boil, uncovered, until reduced by half, about 15 to 20 minutes. Add cream and reduce to 1 cup, about 10 to 15 minutes. Reduce heat to low and add the butter in one chunk and stir constantly until butter melts and is incorporated into sauce. Makes 6 first-course servings.

BASIL-SPINACH-CHICKEN VARIATION In a food processer mince 2 cups well-chilled chicken breast chunks, using several on/off turns; do not overprocess. Add ½ cup well-drained cooked fresh spinach, 1 egg, ⅓ cup fresh bread crumbs (preferably homemade, page 126), 2 tablespoons whipping cream, 1 tablespoon minced fresh basil, ½ teaspoon salt, ¼ teaspoon white pepper and ¼ teaspoon freshly grated nutmeg; process to blend. Chill filling several hours. Proceed with making ravioli as directed above. Makes 2½ cups filling.

FUSILLI WITH TOMATO, ZUCCHINI AND CLAM SAUCE

1 can (10 ounces) baby clams, drained and juice reserved
1 cup whipping cream
2 cups sliced domestic mushrooms
1 medium zucchini, cut in fine julienne
2 tablespoons butter
2 tablespoons olive oil
2 cloves garlic, pressed
2 tomatoes, peeled, seeded and diced
1 pound dried fusilli
¾ cup freshly grated Parmesan cheese

In a small saucepan bring clam juice to a boil; reduce to 3 tablespoons. Add cream to reduced clam juice and bring to a boil. Reduce heat and simmer until reduced to ¾ cup, about 15 to 20 minutes. In a large skillet sauté the mushrooms and zucchini in butter and oil until zucchini is crisp-tender, about 5 to 7 minutes. Stir in the garlic; sauté 1 minute. Add the tomatoes, clams and reduced cream mixture; heat and keep warm. Cook pasta in rapidly boiling, salted water until al dente, 8 to 10 minutes; drain. Combine sauce with cooked fusilli; stir in grated Parmesan cheese. Serve immediately on warm platter. Makes 6 first-course servings.

LOBSTER WITH CHIPOLTE PEPPER CREAM SAUCE

1 cup whipping cream
1 clove garlic, peeled and halved
1 teaspoon chipolte paste (2 tablespoons pureed, canned chipolte-
  chile en adobo)*
1 small hothouse cucumber, scored
  lengthwise with mushroom fluter
  or fork
3 tablespoons butter
1½ cups cooked lobster chunks
  (about 12 ounces)
2 tablespoons chopped fresh
  cilantro
Additional sprigs of cilantro for garnish (about 1 bunch)
2 limes, cut in wedges, for garnish
1 pound Jalapeño Mole Pasta
  (page 131)

In a saucepan bring cream and
garlic to a boil, reduce heat and
simmer until cream is reduced to ¾
cup, about 10 to 15 minutes. Whisk
in the chipolte paste; set aside. Cut
cucumber in half lengthwise and
then into ⅛-inch-thick slices. Measure ½ cup slices for this recipe
(use any remaining cucumber
slices for salads). In a small skillet
sauté cucumber in 2 tablespoons
butter for 2 minutes. Add sautéed
cucumber to reduced cream; keep
sauce warm. Cook pasta in rapidly
boiling, salted water until al dente, 2
to 3 minutes; drain. Meanwhile, in a
small skillet sauté lobster chunks in
remaining butter. Pour cream
sauce over cooked pasta. Add
chopped cilantro and toss lightly.
Divide pasta among 4 plates; top
with sautéed lobster. Garnish with
cilantro sprigs and lime wedges.
Just before eating, squeeze the
lime juice over the pasta. Makes 4
servings.

*Chipolte-chile en adobo is avail-
able at Latin American markets and
well-stocked supermarkets.

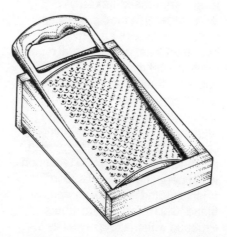

SHRIMP CURRIED EGGS

8 hard-cooked eggs, peeled and
  halved lengthwise
⅓ cup mayonnaise
½ teaspoon paprika
¼ to ½ teaspoon curry powder
¼ teaspoon dry mustard
¼ teaspoon salt
2 cups Sauce Joinville (page 123)
¾ cup cooked bay shrimp
½ cup grated sharp Cheddar
  cheese
½ cup fresh bread crumbs (preferably homemade, page 126)
1 tablespoon melted butter

Remove egg yolks and mash. Add
mayonnaise, paprika, curry powder,
dry mustard and salt; mix well. Stuff
egg whites with mixture and place
in a lightly greased ovenproof casserole. In a medium saucepan heat
Sauce Joinville over medium-low
heat until bubbly. Add shrimp and
cheese and stir until cheese melts;
pour over stuffed eggs. Mix bread
crumbs with the melted butter and
sprinkle over the eggs. Bake in a
350°F. oven until heated through,
about 20 to 25 minutes. Makes 4 to
6 servings.

OMELETTE PICNIC LOAF AUX PROVENCE

1 large round Italian or French bread (10- to 12-inch diameter)
4 tablespoons olive oil
10 ounces mild or hot Italian sausage, casings removed
1 large new potato, cooked and thinly sliced
1 medium onion, finely chopped
1 clove garlic, pressed
1 medium green bell pepper, cored, seeded and chopped
1 medium sweet red bell pepper, cored, seeded and chopped
9 eggs
¾ teaspoon salt
¼ teaspoon freshly ground black pepper

With a serrated knife split bread in half horizontally. Partially hollow center of each half, leaving a 1-inch shell. Brush inside surfaces with 1 tablespoon olive oil. Reassemble loaf, wrap in foil and keep warm in 300°F. oven while preparing omelet.

In a 10-inch omelet pan or skillet crumble sausage and fry until lightly browned. Remove sausage with slotted spoon and drain off fat. In the same skillet sauté potato, onion and garlic in 1 tablespoon olive oil over medium-high heat, stirring often, until nicely browned, about 3 minutes. Add peppers and cook 1 minute longer. Stir in sausage and remove from heat. Whisk the eggs with salt and pepper. Return omelet pan to medium heat and push vegetable mixture to one side. Drizzle 1 tablespoon oil over bottom of pan. Redistribute vegetables in pan and pour in eggs. As the edges begin to set, push mixture toward center and shake pan vigorously to allow uncooked egg to flow underneath. Cook omelet until top is just set but appears moist, and the bottom is lightly browned, about 8 to 10 minutes.

To turn omelet, run a pancake turner around edge and under to loosen. Invert an oiled plate over omelet, and with one hand on the plate, the other hand gripping pan handle, quickly invert pan, turning omelet out onto the plate. Add remaining 1 tablespoon oil to pan, return to medium heat and gently slide omelet back into pan. Cook until lightly browned, about 2 minutes. Remove from heat. Remove bread from oven and open loaf. Invert bottom half of loaf over top of omelet, then quickly invert pan, turning omelet into loaf. Replace top of bread and wrap in several thicknesses of foil to keep warm. Makes 6 servings.

FRESH VEGETABLE OMELET

3 shallots, minced, or ½ cup thinly sliced green onions
½ cup finely minced celery
1 large sweet red or yellow bell pepper, cored, seeded and cut in small strips
3 tablespoons butter
1 cup cooked diced ham or roast beef
8 eggs
3 tablespoons water
2 to 3 tablespoons butter
1 cup grated Swiss cheese
3 tablespoons minced fresh parsley for garnish

In medium skillet sauté shallots, celery and bell pepper in 3 tablespoons butter 5 minutes. Add ham or roast beef; remove from heat and set aside. Whisk eggs and water together.

In large skillet or omelet pan (if nonstick pan is used, less butter is needed) melt 2 tablespoons butter. Pour in the eggs and cook until set. (Lift up cooked portion of egg and allow uncooked egg to run underneath.) Place filling on half of omelet. Sprinkle with half of the cheese. Fold other half of omelet over. Slide omelet onto ovenproof platter. Sprinkle with remaining cheese. Place in warm oven (250°F.) to melt cheese slightly. Garnish with minced parsley. Serve immediately. Makes 4 servings.

ZUCCHINI AND SPINACH FRITTATA

6 zucchini, thinly sliced
4 tablespoons butter
1 onion, peeled and thinly sliced
1 sweet red bell pepper, cored, seeded and diced
2 cups sliced domestic mushrooms
1 bunch fresh spinach, rinsed, dried, stemmed and finely chopped (about 3 cups)
4 eggs
1½ cups half-and-half
½ teaspoon salt
¼ teaspoon freshly ground black pepper
½ teaspoon dried thyme
2 tablespoons chopped fresh basil or 1 teaspoon dried basil, crushed
½ cup freshly grated Parmesan cheese

In a large skillet sauté the zucchini in 2 tablespoons butter; remove zucchini from skillet with a slotted spoon and place in a shallow, greased 2-quart ovenproof casserole. Add 1 tablespoon butter to the skillet and sauté the onion and red bell pepper 5 minutes. Spoon on top of the zucchini. Sauté the mushrooms in the remaining butter 3 minutes; add the spinach and sauté until limp. Spoon on top of the onion-pepper mixture. Whisk the eggs with the half-and-half; mix in the salt, pepper and herbs. Pour over the vegetables, sprinkle with cheese and bake in a 375°F. oven 25 to 30 minutes, or until set. Serve hot, cut in wedges. Makes 6 servings.

ROLLED SOUFFLE WITH SHRIMP AND ASPARAGUS

1 pound fresh asparagus, trimmed and cut in 1-inch lengths and cooked crisp-tender
8 ounces cooked bay shrimp
2 cups Sauce Joinville (page 123)
All-purpose flour
4 tablespoons unsalted butter
⅓ cup all-purpose flour
1¾ cups milk
½ teaspoon salt
¼ teaspoon white pepper
6 large eggs, separated and at room temperature
½ cup freshly grated Parmesan cheese
¼ cup minced fresh parsley
2 tablespoons snipped fresh chives
Sprigs of fresh dill for garnish (1 bunch)

In a medium bowl combine asparagus and shrimp. Add enough Sauce Joinville to bind together for filling (½ to ¾ cup); set aside. Preheat oven to 400°F. Line a greased jelly-roll pan (10 by 15 inches) with greased waxed paper; sprinkle paper with flour and shake off excess. In a heavy saucepan melt the butter, stir in flour and cook, stirring, over moderate heat 2 minutes, or until mixture is light golden. Whisk in the milk vigorously until smooth. Cook until mixture is thickened, stirring constantly, about 5 to 7 minutes. Season with salt and pepper. Whisk the egg yolks and add a small amount of the hot cream sauce to the yolks; return this mixture to the cream sauce. Whisk until blended. Beat the egg whites until firm peaks form. Stir a few large spoonfuls of egg white thoroughly into the sauce, then fold sauce into remaining whites. Fold in ¼ cup grated Parmesan cheese when the whites are nearly combined. Carefully pour the soufflé mixture into the prepared pan. Spread out evenly with a spatula. Sprinkle with the remaining Parmesan cheese. Bake on the center rack of the oven

15 to 20 minutes, or until the soufflé is well-puffed and browned, but not dried out. Just before removing soufflé from oven, heat remaining Sauce Joinville over low heat; keep warm.

Remove soufflé from the oven; sprinkle with the parsley and 1 tablespoon chives. To remove from pan, lay a piece of waxed paper several inches longer than the pan over the soufflé; cover the paper with a baking sheet. Holding pans together, invert. Remove the jelly-roll pan and very carefully peel off the waxed paper. Trim any dry edges, and sprinkle with remaining 1 tablespoon chives. Spread on the filling and gently roll up the soufflé from the short end, lifting the paper to help with the rolling. Place soufflé on a serving platter, or slice and serve on individual plates. Spoon warm sauce over soufflé and garnish with fresh dill sprigs. Makes 6 servings.

FRESH SALMON SOUFFLE WITH LEMON-DILL SAUCE

1 fillet of salmon (8 to 10 ounces), poached (page 86)
3 tablespoons minced shallots
3 tablespoons butter
3 tablespoons all-purpose flour
1 cup milk
½ teaspoon salt
⅛ teaspoon white pepper
1 tablespoon tomato paste
2 teaspoons minced fresh chervil
1 teaspoon minced fresh marjoram
4 egg yolks
½ cup grated Swiss cheese
5 egg whites, at room temperature
1 teaspoon butter
1 tablespoon freshly grated Parmesan cheese
8 to 10 medium cooked and peeled shrimp (optional)

Preheat oven to 375°F. Flake salmon and measure ¾ cup (use remaining salmon for another recipe); set aside. In a large saucepan sauté shallots in butter until tender. Add the flour and cook, stirring, 2 minutes. Remove from heat and whisk in milk, salt, pepper, tomato paste and minced herbs. Return to heat and bring to a boil, whisking constantly. Reduce heat and cook, whisking, for 1 minute; remove from heat. Whisk the egg yolks; stir in Swiss cheese. Add small amount of hot sauce and whisk; return this mixture to sauce and whisk until smooth. Stir in the salmon. In a large bowl beat the egg whites with an electric mixer until stiff, but not dry. Stir one-fourth of the whites into the soufflé base to lighten. With a rubber spatula carefully fold the base into the beaten egg whites.

Butter an ovenproof oval platter or 6-cup soufflé dish; sprinkle with Parmesan cheese. Carefully pour in half of the soufflé mixture; place shrimp on top. Pour remaining soufflé mixture over the shrimp. Set on oven rack placed in middle of oven. Bake 25 to 30 minutes. Serve with Lemon-Dill Sauce. Makes 4 to 6 servings.

LEMON-DILL SAUCE In a medium saucepan melt 2 tablespoons butter; blend in 2 tablespoons all-purpose flour and cook until bubbly and golden. Whisk in 1¾ cups Chicken Stock (page 121); cook, whisking constantly, over medium-low heat, until thick and bubbly. Whisk in 1½ tablespoons fresh lemon juice, 1 to 2 tablespoons snipped fresh dill and ½ teaspoon finely grated lemon peel. Whisk 2 egg yolks and add a small amount of hot sauce to yolks; whisk to blend. Add back to remaining sauce; whisk until smooth. Cook 1 to 2 minutes, continuing to whisk while sauce thickens. Season with salt, if desired.

ITALIAN QUICHE

1 unbaked 10-inch quiche shell
(use Double Crust Pastry, page
127)
3 mild or hot Italian sausages, casings removed
2 to 3 tablespoons olive oil
1 cup sliced domestic mushrooms
1 sweet red bell pepper, cored,
seeded and cut in small strips
2 to 3 shallots, minced
1 garlic clove, pressed
2 to 3 tablespoons olive oil
2 tablespoons chopped fresh basil
¼ teaspoon salt
¼ teaspoon freshly ground black
pepper
3 eggs
1 cup half-and-half
¾ cup shredded mozzarella
cheese

Crumble sausage. In a medium
skillet fry sausage until lightly
browned and all pink color is gone.
Remove sausage with slotted
spoon and drain on paper towels.
Drain fat from skillet and wipe pan
with paper towel. Add 2 tablespoons olive oil and sauté sliced
mushrooms in olive oil until cooked.

Add bell pepper, shallots and garlic;
sauté until soft, 3 to 5 minutes. Use
additional olive oil if needed. Stir in
chopped fresh basil, salt and pepper; remove from heat. Whisk the
eggs. Add half-and-half and whisk
until smooth. Combine sausage
with vegetables and place in pastry
shell; sprinkle with mozzarella
cheese and pour custard mixture
over filling. Bake in a 425°F. oven
30 to 35 minutes, or until custard is
set. Cool 10 minutes. Slice and
serve. Makes 6 to 8 servings.

FRESH CORN TORTILLA CASSEROLE

¾ cup chopped onion
2 tablespoons vegetable oil
1 can (1 pound, 12 ounces) tomatoes with juice, diced
1 tablespoon all-purpose flour
2 teaspoons chili powder
½ teaspoon ground cumin
¼ teaspoon salt or to taste
3 tablespoons prepared salsa
3 ears fresh corn, kernels cut from
cobs
9 corn tortillas, halved, lightly fried
in vegetable oil and blotted with
paper towels
1 pound Monterey Jack cheese,
grated
2 cups sour cream

In a large skillet sauté the onion in
the oil until tender; add the tomatoes, flour, chili powder, cumin, salt,
and salsa. Simmer 10 minutes. Add
the corn and simmer for 5 minutes.
Add more salt, if desired; set sauce
aside to cool. In a 1-quart square
ovenproof casserole or a 9- by 13-
inch baking dish, pour ½ cup
sauce. Arrange 6 tortilla halves
over the sauce. Add one-third of the
remaining sauce, and one-third of
the cheese. Repeat twice, making 3
layers of tortillas. Spread sour
cream over cheese to the edges of
the dish. Bake in 325°F. oven 25 to
30 minutes. Makes 6 main-course
servings or 8 side-dish servings.

NOTE This is a great side dish with
barbecued chicken or steak. Complete the meal with a tossed green
salad.

POACHED CHICKEN BREASTS WITH MUSHROOM, FENNEL AND BELL PEPPER

1 cup Chicken Stock (page 121)
4 slices lemon
2 green onions
Salt to taste
4 whole chicken breasts, halved, skinned and boned
1 pound domestic mushrooms, sliced
1 cup fennel, cut in julienne
1 sweet red bell pepper, roasted, peeled and diced (for roasting technique, see page 126)
1 cup olive oil
3 dried red chile peppers, seeded
1 tablespoon minced garlic
½ cup red wine vinegar
2 teaspoons fennel seed
¾ teaspoon salt
¼ teaspoon freshly ground black pepper
2 bay leaves
½ cup Niçoise olives, pitted and sliced
¼ cup chopped fresh parsley
1 head butter lettuce, leaves separated, for garnish

In a large soup pot heat chicken stock. Add lemon slices, green onions, salt and chicken breasts; poach until cooked through, about 20 to 25 minutes. Cool and chill the chicken in the broth. In a large bowl combine mushrooms, fennel and red pepper.

In a 1-quart saucepan combine oil, hot peppers and garlic and simmer over medium heat until garlic is golden, about 5 minutes. Stir in vinegar, fennel seed, salt, pepper and bay leaves; simmer 3 minutes. Remove from heat and cool slightly; discard bay leaves. Pour dressing over vegetables; toss well. Cover and refrigerate 4 to 24 hours. Combine sliced olives and parsley with vegetables. To serve, place poached breasts in center of an attractive platter. Arrange lettuce leaves around chicken breasts and fill with vegetable mixture. Makes 8 servings.

SZECHWAN CHICKEN SALAD WITH SPICY PEANUT SAUCE

1½ pounds chicken breasts
1 whole green onion, halved
1 slice fresh ginger root, crushed
1 tablespoon dry sherry
½ teaspoon salt
½ teaspoon sugar
3 cups shredded iceberg lettuce for garnish
Spicy Peanut Sauce (following)

In a 2-quart saucepan place chicken, onion, ginger, sherry, salt, sugar and 2 cups water. Bring to a boil, cover, reduce heat and simmer 20 minutes; remove from heat and cool. Strain cooled broth and save for another use. Remove skin from chicken breasts. Shred chicken meat by pulling in long strips; set aside. Arrange shredded lettuce on 6 salad plates. Top lettuce with chicken. Drizzle the Spicy Peanut Sauce over each salad. Makes 6 servings.

SPICY PEANUT SAUCE Whisk together 2½ tablespoons vegetable oil and 1½ tablespoons creamy peanut butter. Whisk in 2 tablespoons soy sauce, 1 tablespoon sugar, 2 teaspoons white vinegar, ½ teaspoon sesame oil, dash of cayenne pepper, 1 tablespoon minced green onion and 1 tablespoon minced fresh cilantro.

CHICKEN, PEAR AND GRAPE SALAD WITH NECTARINE CHUTNEY DRESSING

2 whole chicken breasts, cooked and diced (or cooked meat from 2 ducks)
2 cups cooked wild rice, at room temperature
1 cup finely chopped celery
4 green onions, minced
3 ripe pears, peeled and sliced
1 cup seedless red grapes
Zest of 1 orange, cut fine
1 cup mayonnaise
⅓ cup Nectarine Chutney, cut fine (following) or prepared chutney (see Note)
Salt to taste
Lettuce leaves for garnish
½ cup toasted walnuts or pecans, chopped, for garnish (page 126)

In a large bowl combine diced chicken and rice; add the celery, green onions, pears, grapes and orange zest. Combine the mayonnaise and chutney and toss with the salad; add salt, if needed. Arrange salad in a lettuce-lined bowl or basket lined with plastic wrap and then with lettuce. Garnish with toasted nuts. Makes 8 servings.

NECTARINE CHUTNEY In a 4- to 5-quart acid-resistant saucepan combine 3 pounds peeled and pitted nectarines, cut in ¾-inch chunks; 1 peeled, cored and finely chopped green cooking apple; 1 6-ounce package dried apricots, finely chopped; 1½ cups packed brown sugar; ½ cup currants; 1 cup apple cider vinegar; juice and zest of 2 lemons; juice of 1 orange; ¼ cup finely minced fresh ginger root; 1 finely diced medium onion; 2 pressed garlic cloves; 1 teaspoon salt; ½ teaspoon dry mustard; ¼ teaspoon cinnamon; ¼ teaspoon ground cloves; and ⅛ to ¼ teaspoon cayenne pepper. Cook, covered, over low heat 30 minutes. Remove cover, increase heat to medium and cook, stirring frequently, 30 minutes, or until mixture has thickened. Pour hot chutney at once into hot, sterilized half-pint jars and heat seal (refer to Sterilizing and Sealing Canning Jars, page 126); store in a cool, dry place at least 3 months before using. Makes 7 half-pints.

NOTE Nectarine Chutney needs 3 months' seasoning to blend flavors. A good quality, homestyle, prepared chutney can be substituted. These chutneys are available at gourmet markets and better delicatessens.

CRUNCHY CHICKEN SALAD

2 cups diced cooked chicken
1 can (8 ounces) water chestnuts, drained and sliced
1½ cups finely diced celery
1½ cups chopped peeled apple
½ cup golden raisins
1 cup sour cream
1 cup mayonnaise
2 tablespoons prepared mustard
2 tablespoons drained sweet pickle relish
¼ teaspoon salt

In a large bowl, combine the chicken, water chestnuts, celery, apple and raisins. Combine sour cream, mayonnaise, mustard, pickle relish and salt.

Add dressing to salad and mix thoroughly. Makes 6 salad servings or can be used as a sandwich filling (about 8 sandwiches).

SHRIMP, ARTICHOKE AND PASTA SALAD

1 pound medium cooked shrimp
2 cans (15 ounces each) artichoke
    hearts, drained
⅓ cup sliced green onions
⅔ cup virgin olive oil
⅓ cup fresh lemon juice
½ cup minced fresh parsley
¼ cup snipped fresh dill
4 shallots, minced
2 large cloves garlic, minced or
    pressed
½ teaspoon salt
¼ teaspoon white pepper
1 pound dried pasta (rotelle, fusilli),
    or 1 pound Red Bell Pepper
    Pasta (page 131), cooked,
    drained and tossed with 1 table-
    spoon olive oil
⅓ cup toasted pine nuts for garnish
    (page 126)

In a large bowl combine shrimp, artichoke hearts and green onions. In a medium bowl whisk together olive oil, lemon juice, parsley, dill, shallots, garlic, salt and pepper. Pour the dressing over the shrimp mixture and marinate 15 to 20 minutes. Combine with cooked pasta; chill slightly (pasta salads have more flavor if not chilled for too long). Serve garnished with toasted pine nuts. Makes 8 servings.

PASTA AND SEAFOOD SALAD PROVENCAL

1 pound medium raw shrimp,
    shelled and deveined
¾ pound scallops
6 small squid, cleaned
12 ounces fusilli, cooked, drained
    and tossed with 1 tablespoon
    olive oil
1 medium red onion, finely diced
1 cup frozen petite peas, thawed
1 sweet red bell pepper, cored,
    seeded and cut in ¾-inch strips
⅔ cup olive oil
6 tablespoons fresh lemon juice
Salt and freshly ground black pep-
    per to taste
1½ cups packed fresh basil leaves,
    finely chopped
1 head butter lettuce, leaves sepa-
    rated, for garnish
2 tomatoes, quartered, and ½ cup
    imported olives, sliced, for
    garnish

In a large saucepan, poach shrimp and scallops in water to cover 4 minutes; drain and cool. Set aside. Cut the bodies of the squid into ½-inch circles. Cut tentacles into halves. In a medium saucepan cook squid in 3 cups boiling water for 5 minutes; drain and cool. Combine cooked shrimp, scallops, squid, pasta, onion, peas and bell pepper. In a medium bowl whisk together olive oil and lemon juice. Season with salt and pepper. Toss salad with the dressing and chopped fresh basil. Line salad bowl with butter lettuce leaves. Place salad in bowl and garnish with tomatoes and olive slices. Makes 8 to 10 servings.

CALAMARI VINAIGRETTE

2 pounds squid, cleaned
½ cup finely diced red onion
1 sweet red bell pepper, cored,
    seeded and cut in
    1-inch strips
½ cup frozen petite peas, thawed
Vinaigrette (following)

Cut the bodies of the squid into ½-inch circles. Cut tentacles into halves. In a large saucepan cook squid in 3 cups boiling water 5 minutes; drain and cool. Combine squid, onion, bell pepper and peas in serving bowl. Pour dressing over salad; toss and serve. Makes 4 to 6 first-course or salad servings.

VINAIGRETTE Whisk together ½ cup olive oil, ⅓ cup fresh lemon juice, 1 pressed garlic clove, 2 teaspoons minced fresh dill, 1 teaspoon finely grated lemon peel, ¼ teaspoon salt and ⅛ teaspoon white pepper.

NOTE My daughter and I first sampled a similar appetizer at a favorite waterfront restaurant in San Francisco.

PAELLA SALAD

8 ounces cooked shrimp, peeled and deveined

3 cups cooked saffron rice (see Note), cooled

2 medium ripe tomatoes, cut in small pieces

1½ cups diced cooked chicken

1½ cups diced celery

1½ cups frozen petite peas, thawed

1 can (8 ounces) minced clams, drained

½ cup cored, seeded and diced green bell pepper

½ cup sliced green onions with tops

1 cup mayonnaise

2 tablespoons dry white wine

3 tablespoons drained capers

1 to 2 cloves garlic, minced or pressed

½ teaspoon salt

¼ teaspoon freshly ground black pepper

1 tablespoon fresh lemon juice

6 to 8 large tomatoes cut in decorative tulips for stuffing (page 32)

In a large bowl combine shrimp, rice, tomato pieces, chicken, celery, green peas, clams, green pepper, and onions. In a medium bowl blend mayonnaise, white wine, capers, garlic, salt, pepper and lemon juice. Pour dressing over shrimp mixture and toss lightly; chill. Serve in tomato tulip shells. Makes 6 to 8 servings.

NOTE Cook rice according to package directions. Use chicken stock for the liquid and add a pinch of saffron.

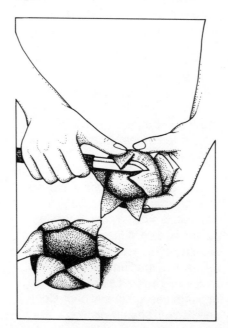

GINGER SHRIMP SALAD

4 tablespoons vegetable oil

2 tablespoons wine vinegar

1 tablespoon fresh lemon juice

¼ teaspoon freshly ground black pepper

½ teaspoon salt

5 slices peeled fresh ginger root (cut ¹⁄₁₆ inch thick)

2 tablespoons finely minced preserved ginger

1 pound medium cooked shrimp, peeled and deveined (or 2 cups shredded cooked chicken)

¼ pound small domestic mushrooms, thinly sliced

8 water chestnuts, thinly sliced

1 small green bell pepper or sweet red bell pepper, cored, seeded and diced

4 green onions (including some of the green tops), cut diagonally in ½-inch pieces

2 cups each shredded lettuce and watercress leaves for garnish

⅓ cup toasted pine nuts for garnish (page 126)

In a small bowl whisk together oil, vinegar, lemon juice, salt, pepper and fresh and preserved ginger. Let sit several hours to blend flavors. Cut shrimp into ½-inch pieces. In a large bowl place shrimp, mushrooms, water chestnuts, diced pepper and green onions; set aside. Arrange shredded lettuce and watercress on a round serving plate. Shake dressing and toss with shrimp mixture. Place shrimp mixture in the center of the lettuce. Sprinkle with pine nuts. Makes 6 servings.

CHINOIS SCALLOP OR SHRIMP SALAD

1 large head red leaf lettuce, 1 bunch arugula or watercress, 1 small head radicchio, washed, dried and torn in bite-sized pieces
Peanut oil
12 fresh shiitake mushrooms (if available) or 12 dried shiitake mushrooms, soaked until softened and drained well*
2 dozen snow peas, strings removed
2 tablespoons salted, fermented black beans, rinsed and mashed (see Note)
1 pound fresh scallops or shrimp
Juice of 2 limes
¼ cup virgin olive oil
1-inch piece of fresh ginger root, peeled and grated (see Note)

2 tablespoons dark soy sauce
1 tablespoon rice vinegar
1 small package enoki mushrooms*, and 1 sweet red bell pepper, cored, seeded and cut into strips, for garnish

Combine greens and set aside. Heat 3 tablespoons peanut oil in wok; add mushrooms and snow peas and stir fry briefly until just tender. Remove with a slotted spoon; set aside. If more oil is needed, add 1 to 2 tablespoons; heat oil. Add mashed black beans if using and stir fry briefly. Add seafood and stir fry 2 to 3 minutes. Return stir-fried vegetables to wok, combine and stir fry 1 minute. Combine lime juice, olive oil, fresh ginger root if using, soy sauce and rice vinegar for dressing. Toss greens with dressing just to coat. Divide among salad plates. Distribute the stir fried seafood and vegetables among the salad plates. Garnish with enoki mushrooms and sweet red bell pepper strips.

*Available at oriental markets and specialty produce markets.

NOTE Flavor the salad *either* with the black beans stir fried with the seafood *or* the ginger added to the dressing. Do not use both.

main courses

BARBECUED FLANK STEAK

1 flank steak (approximately 1 to 1½ pounds)
1 cup unsweetened apple juice
1 cup soy sauce
1 cup vegetable oil
12 to 15 drops liquid smoke
1 bay leaf
2 cloves garlic, pressed
Juice of 2 lemons, strained

Pound flank steak lightly with meat hammer on both sides. In a shallow pan combine apple juice, soy sauce, oil, liquid smoke, bay leaf, garlic and lemon juice. Place steak in marinade, cover and refrigerate at least 3 hours, or up to 6 hours. About 1 hour before serving, remove steak from refrigerator, drain (leftover marinade keeps in the refrigerator 1 week) and let steak come to room temperature. Prepare a barbecue. When coals are hot, grill steak until medium rare, about 5 minutes on each side. Slice in thin strips across the grain of the meat. Makes 4 to 6 servings.

NOTE For a crowd, prepare one recipe marinade for each two flank steaks.

ROLLED SPENCER ROAST WITH BEARNAISE SAUCE AND ARTICHOKES

1 spencer roast (4 to 5 pounds), rolled and tied
3 cloves garlic, peeled and halved
Salt and freshly ground black pepper to taste
1 recipe Béarnaise Sauce (page 123)
1 package (9 ounces) frozen artichoke hearts, cooked and drained

Make 6 small slashes in roast and insert garlic pieces. Season outside of roast with salt and pepper. Place roast on a rack in a roasting pan. Roast in 375°F. oven until medium-rare, approximately 15 to 20 minutes per pound (or until 145°F. on a meat thermometer). When roast is ready, combine cooked artichoke hearts with Béarnaise Sauce. Slice roast and serve with sauce. Makes 6 to 8 servings.

RACK OF LAMB WITH BALSAMIC BEURRE ROUGE

2 racks of lamb (6 to 8 chops on
  each rack)
2 tablespoons butter
1 tablespoon minced shallot
1 to 2 tablespoons minced fresh
  rosemary
Salt and freshly ground black pepper to taste
Fresh sprigs of rosemary for
  garnish
2 tomato roses for garnish (page
  33)
Balsamic Beurre Rouge (following)

Trim most of the fat from the lamb;
score remaining fat. Mix the butter,
shallot and rosemary; spread on
the racks of lamb. Season with salt
and pepper. Place lamb on a rack in
a shallow baking pan. Roast in
425°F. oven 30 minutes. Lamb
should be crisp and brown on the
outside and slightly pink inside.
Serve the racks of lamb on a carving board garnished with fresh
rosemary sprigs and tomato roses.
Accompany with Balsamic Beurre
Rouge. Makes 6 servings.

BALSAMIC BEURRE ROUGE In a
heavy-bottomed saucepan place ½
cup dry red wine (preferably a Ca-
bernet Sauvignon), 3 tablespoons
balsamic vinegar, 2 tablespoons
finely minced shallots and salt and
freshly ground black pepper to
taste. Bring to a gentle boil and
cook until the mixture is reduced to
about 2 tablespoons. Remove from
heat and whisk in 2 tablespoons
chilled unsalted butter (a total of ½
pound chilled unsalted butter will be
needed). Over very low heat whisk
in 14 more tablespoons unsalted
butter, one tablespoon at a time
(sauce should have consistency of
a light hollandaise sauce); stir in 1
to 2 tablespoons minced fresh
rosemary.

SPICY SZECHWAN LAMB AND ASPARAGUS STIR FRY

Marinade (following)
1 pound boneless lean lamb, sliced
  ⅛ inch thick and 1½ inches
  square
Peanut oil
2 tablespoons minced garlic
2 cups fresh asparagus (cut in 1-
  inch pieces on the diagonal)
1 cup toasted cashews or walnuts
  (page 126)
Sauce (following)
Cornstarch paste (½ teaspoon
  cornstarch dissolved in 1 tablespoon water)

Marinate lamb 30 minutes. Heat
wok over high heat until it starts to
smoke; add 2 tablespoons peanut
oil and swirl around sides of pan.
Add the lamb and stir fry until
cooked through and pink color is
gone; remove cooked meat to a
platter and keep warm. Add 2 tablespoons peanut oil to heated wok;
add garlic and stir fry 30 seconds.
Add the asparagus and stir fry until
crisp-tender. Mix in lamb and cashews and stir fry to heat through (if
additional oil is needed add 1 tablespoon while stir frying). Pour Sauce
down sides of the wok and continue
to stir fry. Pour in cornstarch paste;
stir fry 1 minute. Turn out onto a
warm platter and serve immediately. Makes 6 to 8 servings.

MARINADE In a small bowl combine 1 tablespoon light soy sauce, 1
tablespoon mushroom soy sauce, 1
tablespoon oyster sauce, 2 teaspoons cornstarch, 2 teaspoons
peanut oil and 1 teaspoon Shaosing wine or dry sherry.*

SAUCE In a small bowl combine 3
tablespoons Shaosing wine or dry
sherry, 1 tablespoon light soy
sauce, 1 tablespoon mushroom soy
sauce, 1 tablespoon sesame oil, 1
tablespoon minced salted plum, 1
to 2 teaspoons chili paste and ½
teaspoon ground Szechwan pepper.*

*Oriental ingredients available at
oriental markets or well-stocked supermarkets.

SPINACH-STUFFED LEG OF LAMB

½ cup thinly sliced green onions, including some of the green tops
½ cup minced shallots
¼ cup olive oil
2 bunches fresh spinach, rinsed, dried, stemmed and chopped
¼ cup chopped fresh parsley
¼ cup dry bread crumbs (preferably homemade, page 126)
1 egg, lightly beaten
2 tablespoons fresh oregano or 1 teaspoon dried oregano
1 tablespoon fresh thyme or ½ teaspoon dried thyme
2 teaspoons grated lemon peel
Salt and freshly gound black pepper to taste
3 tablespoons butter, softened
2 cloves garlic, minced or pressed
2 tablespoons chopped fresh rosemary
1 leg of lamb (6 to 7 pounds), trimmed, boned and butterflied
4 ounces feta or Bucheron chèvre, crumbled*

In a large skillet sauté onions and shallots in olive oil 5 minutes. Add spinach and parsley and sauté until spinach is limp, about 3 to 5 minutes; remove from heat and cool. Stir in bread crumbs, egg, herbs and lemon peel. Season with salt (sparingly—feta cheese is salty) and pepper. Prepare a paste of the butter, garlic and rosemary. Flatten lamb with a meat hammer (truss if necessary to form a flat, open surface). Spread inside surface with half of the garlic-rosemary paste; cover with spinach filling. Place cheese on top of spinach and press slightly with hand. Roll up meat and tie with kitchen string. Rub outside of rolled lamb with remaining paste. Place on a roasting rack in a roasting pan. Roast in preheated 350°F. oven 1½ to 2 hours, depending on degree of doneness desired (140°F. on a meat thermometer for rare, 145°F. for medium-rare). Remove to serving platter, remove strings, slice and serve. Makes 8 servings.

NOTE   This presentation of lamb was described to me by Ben Zeitman of Amador Foothill Winery. A zinfandel is a nice choice with this hearty lamb dish, and the zinfandels from Amador County are particularly good. The Minty Orange, Onion and Cucumber Salad (page 68) would be a nice accompaniment.

*Available at better cheese shops and some gourmet markets.

VEAL MEDALLIONS WITH STILTON SAUCE AND SHIITAKE MUSHROOMS

1½ cups Beef Stock (page 122)
1½ cups Chardonnay
2 packages (1 ounce each) dried shiitake mushrooms, soaked in warm water for 30 minutes, well drained and stems removed*
3 shallots, peeled and sliced crosswise into thin slices
1 to 2 tablespoons unsalted butter (use least amount possible)
2 tablespoons port or Madeira
1 pound veal medallions (trimmed and cut thin)
2 tablespoons unsalted butter
¾ cup whipping cream
1½ ounces Stilton cheese

In a medium saucepan combine beef stock and Chardonnay and bring to a boil; continue cooking until reduced to 1 cup, about 15 minutes. Set aside. In a large skillet sauté the mushrooms and shallots in butter over low heat until tender, about 20 minutes. Add port or Madeira and cook 2 minutes; remove from skillet and set aside. In the same skillet sauté veal in butter until lightly browned. Remove to ovenproof platter and keep warm in oven. Pour off excess fat from skillet. Add reduced wine mixture and scrape up any browned bits from bottom of skillet.

With an electric mixer in a medium bowl whip cream until soft peaks form. In a large skillet combine half of the whipped cream, the Stilton cheese and the wine reduction and whisk lightly. Heat sauce over low heat. Add remaining whipped cream and stir gently to combine. Add sautéed mushrooms and veal and combine. Veal may be served as a main dish or the sauce and veal may be spooned over cooked pasta or rice. Makes 3 to 4 servings.

*Available at oriental markets or specialty produce markets.

GRILLED VEAL CHOPS WITH FRESH TOMATO-TARRAGON SAUCE

4 veal loin chops (8 ounces each)
2 tablespoons olive oil
2 tablespoons fresh lemon juice
Salt and freshly ground black pepper to taste
Fresh Tomato Tarragon Sauce (following)

Brush veal chops with olive oil. Sprinkle lemon juice on chops and refrigerate 30 minutes. Prepare a barbecue.* When coals are hot grill veal about 3 inches above heat source 5 to 7 minutes on each side (veal should be slightly pink inside). Season lightly with salt and pepper. Nap dinner plates with the Tomato Tarragon Sauce and place veal chops on top. Makes 4 servings.

FRESH TOMATO-TARRAGON SAUCE In a large skillet sauté 2 minced shallots in 2 tablespoons butter until soft, about 8 minutes. Add ½ cup sauvignon blanc and bring to a boil; reduce to ¼ cup, about 6 minutes. Add 6 large peeled, seeded and finely chopped tomatoes and cook 8 minutes. Stir in 2 tablespoons chopped fresh tarragon leaves and season to taste with salt and white pepper.

NOTE The Wild Rice and Porcini Timbales (page 103) are a perfect accompaniment to this dish. The Fresh Tomato-Tarragon Sauce is excellent with grilled veal, chicken or fish, or as a light sauce for pasta.

*Use mesquite charcoal, if possible. Mesquite is available at better cookware stores, gourmet markets, hardware stores and well-stocked supermarkets.

ORIENTAL BARBECUED SPARERIBS

½ cup hoisin sauce*
2 tablespoons oyster sauce*
2 tablespoons mushroom soy sauce*
2 tablespoons Shaosing wine* or dry sherry
1 tablespoon honey
1 tablespoon peanut oil
2 cloves garlic, pressed
1 teaspoon chili paste*
4 pounds pork spareribs (purchase the whole side and leave in one piece)

In a medium bowl combine hoisin sauce, oyster sauce, soy sauce, wine, honey, oil, garlic and chili paste. Brush and rub marinade into spareribs. Place spareribs, meaty side up, on a rack in a large roasting pan. Fill an ovenproof dish with water and place on rack in bottom of oven. Roast ribs in 350°F. oven until meat begins to shrink from bones near bone tip, about 1 hour. Cut into individual servings. Makes 6 to 8 servings.

*Available at oriental markets or well-stocked supermarkets.

PORK OR CHICKEN SATES WITH UDON NOODLES, PEANUT SAUCE AND STIR-FRIED VEGETABLES

1 fresh hot chile, washed, stemmed, seeded and coarsely chopped
1 small onion, peeled and coarsely chopped
2 teaspoons finely minced fresh ginger root
2 tablespoons lime juice
2 tablespoons mushroom soy sauce*
2 tablespoons water
2 pounds boneless pork, cut in 1-inch by ½-inch squares, or 5 chicken breast halves, cut in 1-inch by ½-inch squares
1 package (12 ounces) fresh udon noodles, cooked al dente, drained and coated with 1 tablespoon peanut oil
2 tablespoons peanut oil
1 teaspoon sesame oil
1 clove garlic, finely minced
½ pound green beans, cut in matchstick julienne and blanched
1 sweet red bell pepper, cored, seeded and cut in matchstick julienne
Peanut oil
Peanut Sauce (page 66, prepare double recipe)

In a blender or food processor puree chile, onion, ginger, lime juice, soy sauce and water. Pour mixture into flat baking dish, add pork or chicken and marinate 2 hours in the refrigerator, turning occasionally. Remove pork or chicken from marinade and thread on bamboo skewers (see Note). Prepare a barbecue. When coals are hot grill sates, turning occasionally, until cooked through, about 8 to 10 minutes. Brush with peanut oil if needed while grilling.

While sates are grilling, heat wok over high heat until it starts to smoke. Combine peanut and sesame oils. Add oil to wok and swirl around sides of pan. Add garlic and stir fry 30 seconds. Add green beans and red pepper and stir fry. Remove from heat. In a large bowl combine cooked udon noodles and stir fried vegetables, and toss with half of the Peanut Sauce. Arrange noodle mixture on serving dish or individual plates. When sates are done, arrange on top of noodles (meat may be removed from the skewer or may be left on the skewer). Pass remaining Peanut Sauce in a sauce boat. Makes 6 servings.

NOTE Soak skewers in water for 30 minutes before using.

*Available at oriental markets. Noodles may also be found in the refrigerator section of well-stocked supermarkets.

ROAST PORK WITH ORANGE AND APRICOTS

1 center cut pork loin roast (about 3 pounds)
2 navel oranges
1 cup orange juice
1 cup apricot nectar
1 cup dried apricots
Cornstarch paste (1 tablespoon cornstarch combined with 2 tablespoons cold water)
2 tablespoons Grand Marnier
½ teaspoon salt
⅛ teaspoon freshly ground black pepper

Roast pork on rack in roasting pan in a 325°F. oven for about 1½ hours (or until 165°F. degrees on meat thermometer). Meanwhile, prepare oranges. Remove zest and cut in 1-inch strips. In a small saucepan blanch zest for 10 minutes in simmering water; drain thoroughly and reserve. Remove white membrane from oranges and section oranges; set sections aside. In a medium saucepan combine orange juice and apricot nectar. Add apricots and cook over low heat 10 minutes. Add cornstarch paste to hot mixture, whisking until smooth. Cook 2 minutes over low heat, stirring frequently until mixture thickens. Remove from heat and add Grand Marnier, salt, pepper, zest and orange sections. Remove pork to platter and keep warm. Add ¼ cup water to roasting pan and deglaze, scraping up any browned bits that may have stuck to the bottom of the pan. Add to the sauce and combine; reheat, if necessary. Carve roast and serve with sauce. Pass any remaining sauce in sauce boat. Makes 6 servings.

RASPBERRY CHICKEN WITH CHUTNEY

1 chicken (about 2½ pounds), quartered
½ cup raspberry vinegar
2 teaspoons fresh thyme or ½ teaspoon dried thyme
Salt and freshly ground black pepper to taste
½ cup Nectarine Chutney (page 80) or prepared chutney (see Note)
Zest from 1 orange for garnish

In a large bowl combine chicken pieces, vinegar and thyme; marinate several hours. Arrange chicken pieces in a flameproof baking dish, reserving the marinade. Season chicken with salt and pepper. Spoon chutney over chicken.

Bake in a 325°F. oven 50 minutes, or until done. Transfer chicken to a platter and keep warm. Spoon the fat off of the cooking juices and place baking dish over medium heat. Add the reserved marinade and bring to a boil, scraping up any browned bits from bottom of pan. Reduce sauce until slightly thickened, about 10 minutes. Pour sauce over chicken; garnish with orange zest. Makes 4 servings.

NOTE Nectarine Chutney needs 3 months' seasoning to blend flavors. A good quality, homestyle, prepared chutney can be substituted. These chutneys are available at gourmet markets and better delicatessens.

ROAST CHICKEN WITH ORANGE-MINT BUTTER

1 bunch fresh mint, washed
1 roasting chicken (4 pounds)
4 tablespoons butter, softened
Salt and freshly ground black pepper to taste
3 tablespoons Grand Marnier
¼ cup fresh orange juice
½ cup Chicken Stock (page 121)
6 tablespoons butter, cut in chunks
2 tablespoons chopped fresh mint leaves
Zest of 1 orange, finely cut
Mint sprigs and 2 sliced oranges for garnish

Preheat oven to 400°F. Place 6 sprigs of fresh mint in cavity of chicken and close cavity with a skewer. Make a paste of the butter, salt and pepper; rub paste into the skin of the chicken. Place chicken, breast side up, on a rack in roasting pan; place in oven. Reduce temperature to 350°F. Roast chicken 1 to 1¼ hours, basting every 15 to 20 minutes, or until done. Place cooked chicken on a warm platter and remove mint sprigs; keep chicken warm.

Spoon off excess fat from pan. Over direct heat, deglaze pan with remaining pan juices and Grand Marnier. Add orange juice and chicken stock and bring to a boil, scraping up any browned bits from bottom of pan; transfer liquid to a heavy saucepan. Bring sauce to boil and reduce to ½ cup. Remove from heat and whisk in butter, one piece at a time; add chopped mint and orange zest. Garnish chicken with sprigs of mint and orange slices. Pass sauce in a gravy boat. Makes 4 to 5 servings.

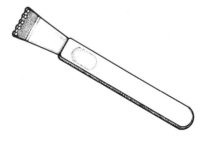

HERBED CHICKEN BREASTS WITH FRESH BABY ARTICHOKES

3 large whole chicken breasts, halved, skinned and boned (page 40)
3 tablespoons olive oil
Additional olive oil
2 medium shallots, finely chopped
1½ pounds baby artichokes (about 16), washed, quartered and tips of leaves trimmed
1 pound Roma tomatoes, peeled, seeded and chopped
2 cloves garlic, pressed
¾ cup white wine
2 tablespoons fresh lemon juice
1 tablespoon finely minced fresh rosemary
1 teaspoon fresh oregano
1 teaspoon fresh thyme leaves (discard woody stem)
½ teaspoon salt
¼ teaspoon freshly ground black pepper
1 tablespoon chopped fresh basil leaves for garnish

In large skillet sauté the chicken in 3 tablespoons olive oil over medium-high heat; turn and brown all sides. Remove to platter. Add 1 tablespoon olive oil to skillet and heat. Sauté shallots 2 minutes; add artichoke quarters and sauté until lightly cooked on all sides (add additional olive oil if needed). Return chicken to skillet. Add tomatoes, garlic, wine, lemon juice, rosemary, oregano and thyme. Bring to a boil, reduce heat and simmer 45 minutes, stirring occasionally. Season with salt and pepper. Arrange chicken breasts on serving platter. Pour over tomato-artichoke sauce. Garnish with basil leaves. Makes 6 servings.

YOGURT CHICKEN WITH ORANGES

3 oranges
4 large whole chicken breasts, halved, skinned and boned (page 40)
2 tablespoons butter
2 tablespoons vegetable oil
1 large onion, chopped
2 cloves garlic, minced or pressed
1 tablespoon sugar
½ teaspoon ground coriander
½ teaspoon ground cumin
1 tablespoon cornstarch
1 cup plain yogurt
Salt and freshly ground black pepper to taste

Remove rind and white membrane from 2 oranges; cut oranges crosswise into slices. Reserve. Remove zest from third orange and cut fine. Squeeze juice from oranges and strain. Measure ¾ cup and set aside. In a large skillet brown chicken in butter and oil on both sides; remove chicken to platter. Add onion and garlic to skillet; sauté 2 minutes. Add chicken, orange juice, zest, sugar, coriander and cumin. Simmer, covered, until chicken is cooked through, about 20 minutes. Mix cornstarch and yogurt; stir into pan juices and cook just until thickened. Season with salt and pepper. Remove chicken to warm platter, cover with sauce and garnish with reserved orange slices. Makes 8 servings.

CHICKEN BREASTS ALSACE

3 whole chicken breasts, halved, skinned and boned (page 40)
2 tablespoons butter
1 tablespoon vegetable oil
⅓ cup chopped shallots
2 tablespoons brandy
1¾ cups Riesling (not too dry)
Bouquet garni (3 sprigs fresh thyme, 2 sprigs fresh parsley and 1 bay leaf tied in a cheesecloth bag)
Salt and freshly ground black pepper to taste
¼ teaspoon freshly grated nutmeg
3 tablespoons butter
1 cup domestic mushrooms
3 tablespoons fresh lemon juice
⅓ cup whipping cream
1 egg yolk

In a large skillet brown chicken in butter and oil on both sides. Reduce heat, add shallots and cook 2 minutes; drain off fat. Add brandy and ignite, shaking pan until flame dies. Add wine, bouquet garni, salt, pepper and nutmeg. Bring to a boil, cover, reduce heat and simmer until

chicken is tender, about 30 minutes. In a separate skillet, melt 3 tablespoons butter. Add mushrooms and lemon juice and cook until tender. With a slotted spoon transfer mushrooms to the skillet containing the chicken. Remove chicken pieces to a warm platter. In a small bowl whip cream and egg yolk. Slowly add to skillet and heat over medium-low heat. Pour mushrooms and sauce over chicken and serve. Makes 6 servings.

PINEAPPLE SHELLS WITH CHICKEN STIR FRY

½ teaspoon salt
1 tablespoon dry white wine
1 teaspoon cornstarch
3 chicken breast halves, skinned, boned (page 40) and cut into cubes
1 medium fresh pineapple
3½ tablespoons peanut oil
1 teaspoon sesame oil
1 tablespoon finely minced fresh ginger root
1 sweet red bell pepper, cored, seeded and cut into strips
12 snow peas, halved crosswise on the diagonal
2 green onions, cut in 1-inch pieces
1½ teaspoons white vinegar
Cornstarch paste (½ teaspoon cornstarch mixed with 2 teaspoons pineapple juice)

In a medium shallow dish combine salt, wine and cornstarch; add chicken and coat with marinade. Quarter the pineapple lengthwise. With grapefruit knife remove flesh from each quarter and cut into small chunks. Reserve shells. Measure 1½ cups chunks for this recipe (use remaining chunks for another recipe). Place pineapple chunks in colander and drain (reserve juice).

Combine oils. Heat a wok over high heat until it begins to smoke; add 2 tablespoons oil and swirl around sides of wok. Add chicken and stir fry until cooked. Remove to platter and keep warm. Add remaining oil to hot wok. Add ginger and stir fry for 30 seconds. Add red bell pepper, snow peas and green onions and stir fry until crisp-tender, about 2 minutes. Return chicken to wok; add pineapple chunks and stir to heat through. Combine vinegar with cornstarch paste and add to wok. Stir fry 2 minutes. To serve, divide stir fry among the four pineapple shells and serve immediately. Makes 4 servings.

SAUTEED MARINATED POUSSIN OR CORNISH HEN

3 tablespoons chopped fresh
  thyme
3 cloves garlic, minced
3 poussins* or Rock Cornish game
  hens, halved
Juice of 2 oranges, strained
Juice of 1 lemon, strained
Juice of 1 lime, strained
2 tablespoons unsalted butter
2 tablespoons olive oil
1 cup dry white wine
6 sprigs fresh thyme
Tomato rose (page 33) and watercress sprigs for garnish

Combine thyme and garlic and rub over chicken halves. Place chicken in a shallow glass baking dish. Combine the citrus juices and pour over the chicken; marinate several hours in the refrigerator, turning at least once. Remove the chicken from the marinade. Strain marinade and save. In a large ovenproof skillet or sauteuse pan brown the chicken in butter and oil on both sides; remove chicken to platter (if there is a large amount of fat, pour off all but 2 tablespoons). Pour ½ cup of the marinade and ½ cup wine into pan. Deglaze pan, stirring up any browned bits from bottom of pan. Return chicken to the pan; add sprigs of fresh thyme. Roast chicken in a 400°F. oven 15 to 20 minutes, or until done. (If marinade cooks down as the chicken roasts, add additional marinade.) Remove from oven and place roasted chicken on a warm platter; discard thyme. Place skillet over direct heat, add ½ cup wine and cook until reduced to a nice glaze, about ¼ cup. Pour glaze over the chicken. Garnish with a tomato rose and watercress sprigs. Makes 6 servings.

*Poussins are baby chickens that weigh approximately 1 pound. They are available at poultry markets.

GAME HENS NORMANDY

3 tart apples, peeled, cored and cut
  in wedges
5 tablespoons butter
3 Rock Cornish game hens, halved
¼ teaspoon salt
⅛ teaspoon white pepper
½ cup half-and-half
⅓ cup Calvados
Orange twists for garnish (page 34)

In a large skillet sauté apple wedges in 3 tablespoons butter for 3 minutes; remove wedges with slotted spoon and set aside. Brown hens in remaining butter on both sides. In a large ovenproof sauteuse pan or casserole arrange hens and add cooked apples; sprinkle with salt and pepper. Cover tightly and bake in a 350°F. oven 45 minutes, or until hens are tender. Pour half-and-half over hens and bake an additional 5 minutes. Just before serving, heat Calvados and pour over hens. Ignite, let flame burn a few seconds, then extinguish with pan lid. Place hens on a serving dish and garnish with orange twists. Pass the sauce in a gravy boat. Makes 6 servings.

GRILLED HIBISCUS CORNISH HENS

3 Rock Cornish game hens, halved and backbones removed
1 cup dried hibiscus flowers*
1 cup sauvignon blanc
2 cloves garlic, minced
8 sprigs fresh cilantro
2 tablespoons olive oil
1 large lime, sliced
2 tablespoons packed brown sugar
3 tablespoons fresh pineapple puree (about ⅓ of a fresh pineapple, peeled, cored and pureed in a blender)
Optional garnish: Leaves from 1 head red leaf lettuce, ⅔ fresh pineapple, peeled and cut into spears and well-washed fresh red hibiscus flower petals

Flatten hens slightly. In a small saucepan combine ½ cup dried hibiscus and wine; simmer 10 minutes. Strain and discard hibiscus. In a small bowl combine hibiscus-flavored wine, garlic, cilantro, olive oil and lime slices. Place Cornish hens in large shallow dish and pour hibiscus marinade over the birds. Marinate in the refrigerator 3 to 6 hours, turning occasionally.

To prepare glaze combine ¾ cup water, ½ cup dried hibiscus flowers and brown sugar in a small saucepan. Bring to a boil, reduce heat and simmer 10 minutes; strain and discard hibiscus. Stir in pineapple puree.

Prepare a barbecue.* When coals are hot, remove hens from marinade and grill 15 to 20 minutes, turning as needed. Brush with glaze several times during grilling. To serve, arrange lettuce on individual plates. Place a grilled hen half on lettuce and garnish with pineapple spears and hibiscus petals, if desired. Makes 6 servings.

NOTE This recipe is an adaptation of a presentation prepared by Mark Miller at the Fourth Street Grill, Berkeley, California. Mark used quail instead of Rock Cornish game hens.

*Dried hibiscus flowers are available at Latin American markets or well-stocked supermarkets.

Use mesquite charcoal, if possible. Mesquite is available at better cookware stores, gourmet markets, hardware stores and well-stocked supermarkets.

TEA-SMOKED DUCK CHINOIS

1 duckling (4 pounds)
1 teaspoon salt
1 tablespoon Szechwan
   peppercorns*
2 tablespoons dry sherry
¼ cup raw white rice
¼ cup packed brown sugar
¼ cup black tea leaves (Jasmine
   recommended)
Zest from 1 orange, coarsely
   chopped
2 whole green onions
6 slices fresh ginger root (about 1½
   inches in diameter)
Plum Blossom Sauce (following)
Garlic chives* or green scallions
   and 6 kumquat flowers (page 35)
   for garnish

Rinse duck inside and out; pat dry. Pierce skin several times with a fork. In a small cast iron frying pan cook the salt and the peppercorns over medium-low heat, shaking pan often until salt begins to brown and peppercorns become fragrant, about 10 minutes. Cool mixture and then grind in a blender or with a mortar and pestle. Strain to remove peppercorn hulls. Combine strained mixture with sherry and use to rub inside and outside of duck.

Line a wok (do not use an electric wok) or a pan with a high, domed lid with aluminum foil; add the rice, brown sugar, tea leaves and orange zest. Stir to mix. Place a round cake rack or steamer in the wok so that it sits 1 inch above the rice mixture; set duck on rack. Cook over high heat. When rice mixture begins to smoke, cover pan tightly and smoke 5 minutes. Reduce heat to medium and smoke 15 minutes (do not open lid). Remove from heat and let sit, covered, for 15 minutes; remove duck. Discard rice mixture.

Insert the onions and the ginger into the cavity of the duck. Place duck, breast side down, on a rack in a roasting pan. Roast in 375°F. oven 1 hour. Drain and discard fat from pan. Turn duck over; return to oven and bake 30 minutes, or until duck is cooked to desired doneness. Remove from oven. Increase oven temperature to 450°F. Drain fat from roasting pan. Return duck to oven and roast just until skin is crisp, about 5 minutes. Slice breast meat in thin slices and slice meat from legs, or cut duck in quarters. Serve with Plum Blossom Sauce and garnish with garlic chives and kumquat flowers. Makes 3 to 4 servings.

PLUM BLOSSOM SAUCE In a blender or food processor puree 1½ pounds halved and pitted fresh plums (or a 17-ounce can purple plums, drained and plums pitted), ½ cup Chinese plum wine and 1 coarsely chopped onion. In a large saucepan add plum puree, 1 6-ounce can thawed frozen lemonade concentrate, ⅓ cup catsup or chili sauce, ¼ cup soy sauce, 1 table-spoon grated fresh ginger root, 2 teaspoons prepared mustard and 2 drops hot pepper sauce; simmer 15 to 20 minutes.

*Available at oriental markets or specialty produce markets.

POACHED SALMON WITH LEMON-CUCUMBER-DILL SAUCE

½ cup dry white wine
1 bay leaf
4 slices lemon
3 large salmon fillets, boned (see
   Note) and halved
1 small cucumber, scored with a
   mushroom fluter or fork and cut
   lengthwise and then crosswise
   into crescents for garnish
Lemon-Cucumber-Dill Sauce
   (following)

In a pan (with lid) big enough to hold the salmon combine 1 cup water, wine, bay leaf and lemon slices. Bring to a simmer and add salmon. Poach, covered, until salmon flakes when tested (salmon may be chilled in poaching liquid). Remove salmon from poaching liquid. Garnish with cucumber crescents and serve with Lemon-Cucumber-Dill Sauce. Makes 6 servings.

LEMON-CUCUMBER-DILL SAUCE In a medium bowl combine 1 cup sour cream, 2 tablespoons fresh lemon juice, 2 tablespoons snipped fresh dill, 1 tablespoon prepared horseradish, 1 tablespoon grated onion and ½ teaspoon celery salt. Stir in 1 peeled and finely diced hothouse cucumber; chill several hours.

NOTE A strawberry huller works well for removing fish bones.

SALMON FILLETS WITH TANGERINE AND GINGER BEURRE BLANC

6 butter lettuce leaves
3 large salmon fillets (8 to 10 ounces each), each boned (see Note), skinned and cut in 2 pieces
Vegetable oil
¼ cup white wine
1 tablespoon white wine vinegar
3 tablespoons finely minced shallots
1 tablespoon thawed frozen tangerine juice concentrate (see Note)
1 tablespoon fresh ginger essence (prepare by pressing slices of fresh ginger root in a garlic press)
½ pound well-chilled unsalted butter, cut in 16 pieces
1 tablespoon tangerine zest (see Note)
18 green onion fans, each 2 inches long (page 36)

To steam salmon: Place 1 to 1½ inches water in a wok and bring to a boil. Line bamboo steamer trays with lettuce leaves. Brush one side of each salmon fillet lightly with oil (this prevents salmon from sticking). Place fillets, oiled side down, on lettuce-lined steamer tray. Stack bamboo steamer and place over boiling water in wok. Reduce heat and steam salmon fillets 8 to 10 minutes, or until cooked through (watch the level of the water so wok

does not boil dry; add additional water if needed).

While salmon is steaming, prepare sauce. In a small, heavy-bottomed saucepan combine wine, vinegar and shallots and boil over medium-high heat until reduced to 2 tablespoons, 8 to 10 minutes. Add the tangerine juice and ginger essence. Remove saucepan from heat. Whisk in 2 pieces of butter until just incorporated. Place saucepan over very low heat and whisk in remaining butter, one piece at a time, adding each piece only after the previous piece is nearly incorporated; sauce should be thick and emulsified. Remove sauce from heat (strain for extra smoothness); stir in zest from the tangerine. To serve, divide sauce between 6 plates. Place a piece of steamed salmon on the sauce. Garnish with green onion fans, 3 per plate. Makes 6 servings.

NOTE Frozen orange juice concentrate and orange zest may be substituted if tangerine is unavailable.

Many people prefer beer with oriental cuisine, but try a dry Gewurztraminer. The spicy character of this wine goes well with oriental foods.

BROILED OR GRILLED SALMON WITH FENNEL SAUCE

3 large salmon fillets (8 to 10
   ounces each), each boned (see
   Note), skinned and cut in 2
   pieces
2 tablespoons vegetable oil
1 head fresh fennel (about 1 pound)
5 tablespoons butter, softened
Salt to taste
⅛ teaspoon cayenne pepper
¼ teaspoon freshly grated nutmeg
Vegetable oil
Fennel sprigs for garnish

Preheat broiler or prepare a barbecue. Brush salmon with oil. Trim the
fennel and use the tender inner part
of the bulb. Cut bulb into cubes and
measure 1½ cups. In a medium
saucepan combine fennel, ⅓ cup
water and 1 tablespoon butter; cook
5 minutes. Pour the mixture into a
food processor or blender and add
the remaining butter; puree. Pour
the puree into a small saucepan;
add the salt, cayenne pepper and
nutmeg. Simmer 3 minutes.
   Broil or grill salmon approximately 4 to 5 minutes on each side
(depending on thickness); brush
with oil as needed. Serve salmon
with the fennel sauce and garnish
with fennel sprigs. Makes 6 servings.

NOTE A strawberry huller works
well for removing fish bones.

GRILLED SALMON WITH RED BELL PEPPER-BASIL BUTTER

½ cup olive oil
2 tablespoons chopped fresh basil
4 salmon fillets (6 ounces each),
   skin removed
Red Bell Pepper-Basil Butter
   (following)

Mix the olive oil and chopped basil.
Place the salmon fillets in a shallow
glass baking dish and cover with
the olive oil mixture. Cover and
marinate in the refrigerator at least
2 hours. Prepare a barbecue.*
When coals are hot grill salmon fillets 4 to 5 minutes on each side
(depending on thickness); baste
with olive oil if needed. Serve immediately with Red Bell Pepper-
Basil Butter. Makes 4 servings.

RED BELL PEPPER-BASIL BUTTER
In a medium heavy saucepan melt
2 tablespoons unsalted butter;
when foam subsides add 2½ cored
and seeded sweet red bell peppers
cut in half-inch pieces and 3 tablespoons minced shallots and sauté
until peppers are tender, about 8
minutes. Add 3 tablespoons raspberry vinegar; cook over low heat
until liquid is reduced by two-thirds,
about 5 minutes. Add ½ cup dry
white wine and ¼ cup fresh lemon
juice and cook over low heat until
liquid is reduced by half, about 15
minutes. Remove from heat; transfer mixture to blender and puree.
Return puree to saucepan. Over
very low heat whisk in ¾ pound
chilled unsalted butter in 12 pieces,
one piece at a time, waiting until
one piece is completely incorporated before adding the next piece.
If a very smooth sauce is desired,
press sauce through a fine mesh
sieve after all the butter has been
added. Stir in ⅓ cup chopped fresh
basil and season with salt, if desired. Serve immediately or keep
warm in a hot water bath up to 1
hour.

*Use mesquite charcoal, if possi-
ble. Mesquite is available at better
cookware stores, gourmet markets,
hardware stores and well-stocked
supermarkets.

GRILLED SWORDFISH WITH CORN AND CILANTRO SAUCE

4 tablespoons olive oil
Juice of 1 lemon, strained
6 swordfish steaks (each 1 inch thick)
Freshly ground black pepper to taste
1¼ cups whipping cream
1 clove garlic, pressed
¼ teaspoon dried red pepper flakes
4 cups fresh corn kernels (about 6 large ears of corn)
2 tablespoons chopped fresh cilantro
Salt to taste
Carrot flowers (page 34) and sprigs of fresh cilantro for garnish

Combine olive oil and lemon juice; brush swordfish with this mixture. Season with pepper and set aside. In a medium saucepan combine the cream, garlic and pepper flakes; bring to a boil over medium-high heat. Reduce heat and simmer until reduced to 1 cup, about 10 minutes. Add corn and simmer until corn is tender, about 5 minutes.

Transfer mixture to a blender or food processor and puree; strain puree through a sieve (see Note). Reheat sauce, stir in cilantro and season with salt.

Prepare a barbecue.* When coals are hot grill swordfish 5 minutes on one side. Turn and brush with olive oil and grill an additional 5 to 8 minutes, or until fish flakes. Serve with corn and cilantro sauce. Garnish with carrot flowers and cilantro sprigs. Makes 6 servings.

NOTE If you prefer a sauce with more texture, omit straining.

*Use mesquite charcoal, if possible. Mesquite is available at better cookware stores, gourmet markets, hardware stores and well-stocked supermarkets.

FILLET OF SOLE WITH ASPARAGUS MALTAISE

16 to 24 fresh asparagus spears, trimmed
8 fillets of sole
5 tablespoons butter, melted
3 egg yolks
2 tablespoons fresh orange juice
2 tablespoons grated orange peel
¼ teaspoon salt
Pinch white pepper
¼ pound butter, melted
1-inch strips of zest from 1 orange for garnish

Place asparagus on rack over boiling water and steam 5 minutes, or until barely tender. Place 2 to 3 asparagus spears on each fillet. Roll the sole around the asparagus, leaving bottoms and tops of asparagus extending out. Place the rolled fillets in an ovenproof baking dish, seam side down. Pour the melted butter over fillets. Cover with aluminum foil and bake in 350°F. oven 20 minutes. Remove from the oven and drain juices; keep warm.

While sole is baking, prepare sauce. Place the egg yolks, orange juice, orange peel, salt and pepper in a blender. Blend at high speed 1 minute. Remove the center cap of the blender lid and with motor running, slowly pour in the melted butter. Keep the sauce warm in a small thermos bottle, or in a double boiler over hot, but not simmering or boiling, water. Serve fillets with Maltaise sauce; garnish with orange zest. Makes 8 servings.

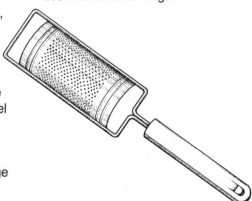

SHRIMP A LA RAIMUND

24 large raw Spanish or regular
shrimp, shelled and deveined
1 large red onion, cut in ¾-inch
pieces
2 large green bell peppers, cored,
seeded and cut in ¾-inch pieces
1 cup olive oil
1 teaspoon chopped fresh
rosemary
1 teaspoon chopped fresh
marjoram
1 teaspoon chopped fresh thyme
3 bay leaves
2 cloves garlic, pressed
3 tablespoons fresh lemon juice
1 teaspoon Worcestershire sauce
3 tablespoons butter
Additional butter if needed
½ cup julienne strips of white onion
⅓ cup dry white wine
Dash of hot pepper sauce
½ cup julienne strips of pineapple
½ cup julienne strips of tomato
(peel and remove seeds)
¼ cup julienne strips of fresh ginger
root
½ cup tequila
1 tablespoon minced fresh parsley
1 teaspoon snipped fresh dill
Salt and freshly ground black pepper to taste

On 6 long wooden skewers alter-
nate shrimp with pieces of onion
and green pepper. In a large bowl
combine olive oil, rosemary, marjoram, thyme, bay leaves, garlic,
lemon juice and Worcestershire
sauce. Marinate shrimp in this mixture in the refrigerator several hours
or overnight; drain shrimp.

In a large skillet sauté shrimp in
butter until they begin to brown
lightly on the edges (don't overcook). Remove from skillet and
keep warm on a covered platter.
Add additional butter to skillet if
needed and sauté onion 3 minutes.
Deglaze pan with wine and add
pepper sauce. Add pineapple, tomato and ginger. Pour tequila over
the top and ignite. Stir in parsley
and dill. Season with salt and pepper, if needed. Divide shrimp
among 6 dinner plates. Spoon
sauce over each serving of shrimp.
Makes 6 servings.

NOTE This recipe is an adaptation
of one presented by Chef Raimund
Hofmeister at the Epicurean Gala in
Los Angeles. The recipe and Exec-
utive Chef Raimund were the hit of
the celebrity cooking demonstra-
tions.

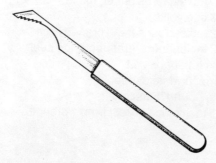

PAELLA

1 chicken (2 ½ to 3 pounds), cut up
¾ pound large or medium raw
shrimp
1 lobster tail (if frozen, thaw)
3 tablespoons olive oil
1 green bell pepper, cored, seeded
and finely minced
1 large onion, finely minced
3 large tomatoes, peeled and
chopped
2 cups raw long grain white rice
¼ teaspoon Hungarian paprika
2 cloves garlic, pressed
8 clams or mussels, well scrubbed
1 cup dry white wine or water
3 cups Chicken Stock (page 121)
1 cup fresh or frozen peas
Pinch saffron
½ pound squid, cleaned and cut
crosswise into circles
3 tablespoons chopped fresh parsley for garnish

In paella pan or large sauteuse pan
cook chicken, shrimp and lobster in
olive oil until chicken and fish are
golden; remove seafood. Add
green pepper and onion; sauté until
tender. Add tomatoes and rice and
cook until juice from tomatoes is reduced, about 10 minutes. Stir in paprika and garlic; remove from heat.
In a separate saucepan steam
clams in the wine until they open
(discard any clams that do not

open). Remove clams and set aside. Strain clam liquor through several thicknesses of cheesecloth in fine sieve. Add the liquor, chicken stock, peas and saffron to the paella pan; bring to a boil, reduce heat and simmer until rice is tender. Return shellfish, add squid and cook 5 minutes. Add clams and cook 2 minutes. Serve in large soup bowls. Sprinkle with parsley. Makes 6 to 8 servings.

OYSTERS WITH SPINACH PUREE AND CIDER BEURRE BLANC

36 unshucked oysters, scrubbed
Rock salt
1 bunch fresh spinach, rinsed, stemmed, cooked and drained
1 tablespoon whipping cream
½ cup hard cider
⅓ cup bottled clam juice
2 tablespoons white wine vinegar
⅓ cup minced shallots
¼ pound butter, cut in pieces
½ cup whipping cream
Salt and white pepper to taste
2 tablespoons snipped fresh chives or minced fresh parsley for garnish

Shuck oysters (page 39). Reserve the shell with the larger round area. Place oysters on plate and set aside. Strain oyster liquor through sieve lined with double layer of cheesecloth and reserve. Line bottom of a jelly-roll pan with a ¼-inch layer of rock salt. In a blender or food processor puree spinach with cream; set aside. In a heavy-bottomed saucepan simmer reserved oyster liquor, cider, clam juice, vinegar and shallots over medium heat until reduced to ½ cup, about 10 minutes. Over low heat whisk in butter, one piece at a time; strain sauce through fine sieve.

In a separate saucepan reduce cream to ¼ cup; whisk into sauce. Season with salt and pepper. To serve, spoon ½ teaspoon sauce and ½ teaspoon spinach into each oyster shell. Top with an oyster and 2 teaspoons sauce. Arrange filled shells on prepared jelly-roll pan. Broil oysters 4 inches from heat, watching carefully, until sauce is bubbly. Garnish with chopped chives or parsley. Makes 6 servings.

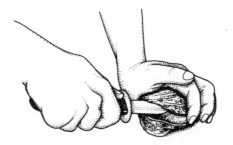

OYSTERS ON THE HALF SHELL WITH MUSTARD SAUCE

½ cup mayonnaise
½ cup sour cream or Crème Fraîche (page 124)
2 tablespoons minced green onion
1 tablespoon capers, rinsed
1 tablespoon minced fresh parsley
2 teaspoons coarse-grained Dijon-style mustard
1 tablespoon fresh lemon juice
Dash of hot pepper sauce
36 unshucked oysters, scrubbed
Cracked ice

Prepare sauce in advance to allow flavors to blend. Combine all ingredients except for oysters and ice in a blender or food processor; puree. Refrigerate until ready to use. To serve, place oysters on a bed of cracked ice. Serve with several oyster knives (see page 39 for instructions for shucking oysters). Makes 6 servings.

NOTE Other sauces that will go well with raw oysters are Salsa Picante Dip (page 45) and Watercress Dip (page 44). Dips may need to be thinned slightly with cream.

accompaniments

GREEN BEANS SESAME

1 pound fresh green beans,
  trimmed and cut diagonally in
  1½-inch pieces
2 teaspoons salt
1 tablespoon peanut oil
2 teaspoons sesame oil
1 to 2 tablespoons toasted sesame
  seeds (page 126)

Bring 4 quarts water to a boil; add
green beans and 2 teaspoons salt.
Cover and return to a boil. Cook
beans until crisp-tender, about 5 to
7 minutes; drain. Heat a large skillet
or wok over high heat. Combine
peanut oil and sesame oil and add
to pan. Briefly stir fry green beans.
Add toasted sesame seeds and stir
fry for an additional minute. Makes
4 servings.

BEETS WITH CARROT PUREE

12 medium fresh beets
1 bunch carrots, cut in 1-inch
  pieces
2 tablespoons butter
Salt and white pepper to taste

Cook beets in water to cover until
tender; drain and cool slightly. Remove beet skin. With melon baller,
scoop a small hole in the top of
each beet. For carrot puree, in a
medium saucepan cook carrots in a
small amount of water until very
tender; drain. Puree carrots, butter
and salt and pepper in a food processor. (Or, puree in a food mill and
mix with butter, salt and pepper.)
Keep puree warm in a double boiler
over hot water. When ready to
serve fill beets with carrot puree.
Makes 6 servings.

FRESH CORN CASSEROLE

2 cups fresh corn kernels (about 3
  large ears of corn)
¼ pound butter, melted
2 eggs
1 cup sour cream
1 cup diced Monterey Jack cheese
½ cup cornmeal
1 can (4 ounces) diced green chiles
½ teaspoon salt

Grease a 2-quart ovenproof casserole. In a blender or food processor puree
1 cup corn kernels with the butter and eggs. In a large mixing bowl combine remaining 1 cup corn kernels, sour cream, cheese, cornmeal, green chiles and salt. Add pureed mixture and blend well. Pour into greased casserole and bake, uncovered, in a 375°F. oven 50 to 60 minutes, or until set. Makes 6 servings.

BAKED STUFFED TOMATOES

6 firm ripe tomatoes
Salt
5 green onions (white part only), thinly sliced
¼ cup olive oil
1 bunch spinach, rinsed, dried, stemmed and coarsely chopped
¼ cup chopped fresh parsley
¼ cup snipped fresh dill or 2 teaspoons dried dill
Freshly ground black pepper to taste
½ cup Bulgarian feta cheese

Slice ½ inch from top of each tomato. With melon baller or tomato corer scoop out pulp and seeds; discard seeds. Chop and reserve pulp. Lighly salt tomato cavities and let drain upside down on paper towels. In a large skillet sauté onions in olive oil until tender. Add tomato pulp, spinach, parsley, dill and pepper. Cook, uncovered, over high heat until most of the liquid is absorbed, about 5 minutes. Remove from heat and stir in all but 2 tablespoons of the cheese; set aside to cool.

Lightly grease baking dish large enough to hold tomatoes. Fill tomato shells lightly with stuffing; sprinkle with remaining feta cheese. Place tomatoes in baking dish and bake in a 375°F. oven until they are cooked through but not splitting open, about 15 to 20 minutes. Makes 6 servings.

HOT AND SOUR ZUCCHINI

2 tablespoons peanut oil
1 tablespoon sesame oil
2 dried red peppers
1 teaspoon Szechwan peppercorns*
1 tablespoon minced fresh ginger root
3 zucchini, sliced in ¼-inch rounds
1 sweet red bell pepper, cored, seeded and cut in small strips
1 tablespoon minced green onion
1 teaspoon cornstarch
1 tablespoon Chinese red vinegar or rice vinegar*
1 teaspoon soy sauce
2 teaspoons sugar

Combine peanut and sesame oils. Heat wok or heavy skillet over high heat until it starts to smoke; add oil and swirl around sides of pan. Add the red peppers and peppercorns to the oil and stir fry 1 minute; remove with skimmer. Add the ginger and stir fry 30 seconds. Add the zucchini, bell pepper and green onion and stir fry until crisp-tender, about 3 minutes. Whisk together the cornstarch, vinegar, soy sauce and sugar. Pour over the stir-fried vegetables; stir fry 1 minute. Transfer to serving dish and serve immediately. Makes 6 servings.

NOTE This is a good accompaniment to roasted or grilled meats, poultry or fish, as well as Chinese dishes.

*Available at oriental markets and well-stocked supermarkets.

SPINACH TIMBALES

⅓ cup minced shallots
2 tablespoons butter
2 large bunches fresh spinach, rinsed, stemmed and finely chopped
¼ teaspoon salt
⅛ teaspoon white pepper
⅛ teaspoon freshly grated nutmeg
2 tablespoons butter
3 eggs
1 egg yolk
1 cup milk
⅔ cup homemade French bread crumbs (page 126; use bread that is several days old and dry)
½ cup grated Gruyère cheese
6 pimiento strips for garnish

In a large saucepan sauté the shallots in the butter until translucent. Add the chopped spinach and cook until tender. Stir in the salt, pepper, nutmeg and additional butter. Set aside. In a large bowl beat eggs and egg yolk until well combined. Slowly add milk and continue beating. Add the spinach mixture, bread crumbs and cheese, and stir to combine. Butter 6 timbale molds or custard cups and fill two-thirds full with the spinach mixture. Set molds in a large, deep baking pan. Fill pan with boiling water halfway up the sides of the molds; place in bottom third of oven. Bake in a 350°F. oven 25 to 30 minutes, or until custard is set. Remove timbales from baking pan and let sit 5 minutes. Unmold timbales by running a knife around the edge. Invert onto serving plate or individual dinner plates, and garnish with pimiento strips. Makes 6 servings.

STIR-FRIED VEGETABLES FOR GRILLED BEEF

1 sweet red bell pepper, cored, seeded and cut in strips
1 yellow bell pepper, cored, seeded and cut in strips
2 zucchini, cut in ¼-inch rounds
1 red onion, cut in chunks
3 tablespoons olive oil
2 tablespoons balsamic vinegar

In a large skillet or wok stir fry vegetables in olive oil until crisp-tender. Add vinegar and stir to mix. Serve with slices of grilled steak. Makes 4 servings.

NOTE Try to find the yellow pepper when in season. An additional red pepper or a green pepper may be used when yellow peppers are not available.

CORN AND CILANTRO FRITTERS

1 cup masa harina* (corn flour)
1 cup beer
3 eggs
1¼ cup fresh corn kernels (about 2 large ears of corn)
½ teaspoon salt
1 jalapeño pepper, seeded and finely minced
2 tablespoons minced fresh cilantro
2 tablespoons unsalted butter
2 tablespoons olive oil
Salsa Supreme (page 124) for accompaniment

Place masa harina in a medium mixing bowl. Slowly add beer and whisk until smooth. Whisk in the eggs. Stir in the corn, salt, jalapeño and cilantro. In a large, heavy-bottomed skillet melt butter over medium-high heat; add the olive oil. When mixture is hot, drop 1 to 2 tablespoons batter for each fritter into the skillet. Cook 1 to 2 minutes, or until golden; turn and cook 1 to 2 minutes more. Remove with slotted spatula or spoon, and drain on paper towels. Keep warm in oven as you fry remaining fritters. Serve with Salsa Supreme. Makes 24 to 28 fritters, or 6 to 8 servings.

* Available at Latin American markets and well-stocked supermarkets.

PARMESAN POTATO FRITES

6 large potatoes
1 quart oil for deep fat frying
½ cup freshly grated Parmesan
　cheese

Peel potatoes and halve. With melon baller cut small potato balls (use leftover potato pieces for another recipe). In a deep frying pan or large saucepan heat oil to 375°F. Add potato balls (about 15 to 20) and deep fry 5 to 7 minutes, or until golden brown. Remove potato balls with slotted spoon or skimmer and drain on paper towels. While still hot, roll in Parmesan cheese and serve immediately. Makes 4 servings.

WEHAHOMA RICE PILAF

2 cups Chicken Stock (page 121)
Salt to taste
1 cup wehahoma rice*
⅓ cup minced green onion (including some of the green tops)
4 tablespoons butter
½ cup pecans, toasted and chopped (page 126)

In 2 quart saucepan bring the stock to a boil (add salt, if needed). Stir in the rice and return to boil. Reduce heat and cook, covered, 35 to 40 minutes; cool to room temperature. In a large skillet sauté minced green onion in butter; stir in cooked rice and pecans and heat through. Makes 6 servings.

*Wehahoma rice is a brown rice grown in northern California. It is long grained and has a rough texture much like wild rice. It is available at some health food stores and is also called wehani rice. Regular brown rice may be substituted in this recipe.

WILD RICE AND PORCINI TIMBALES

2 ounces dried porcini mushrooms*
2 tablespoons unsalted butter
1 tablespoon minced shallots
3 eggs
1 egg yolk
1½ cups half-and-half
½ cup cooked wild rice (cook according to package directions using chicken stock for the liquid)
½ teaspoon salt
¼ teaspoon finely ground white pepper
⅛ teaspoon nutmeg
2 tablespoons finely minced fresh parsley

Rinse the mushrooms to remove any excess dirt and grit. Soak the mushrooms in warm water for at least 30 minutes. Drain, saving the liquid. Slice the mushrooms into ¼-inch strips. Strain the soaking liquid through coffee filter paper or two thicknesses of fine cheesecloth. Reserve liquid. In a small skillet sauté mushrooms in the butter. Deglaze pan with the reserved soaking liquid and continue cooking until all moisture is evaporated, about 10 minutes. Remove from heat and cool.

In a large mixing bowl beat eggs and egg yolk until well blended. Slowly add half-and-half and mix. Add the wild rice, salt, pepper, nutmeg, fresh parsley and mushroom strips. Butter 6 timbale molds or custard cups and fill two-thirds full with the custard and mushroom mixture, distributing the mushrooms evenly. Set molds in a large, deep baking pan. Fill pan with boiling water halfway up the sides of the molds; place in bottom third of oven. Bake in a 350°F. oven 25 to 30 minutes, or until custard is set. Remove timbales from baking pan and let sit 5 minutes. Unmold timbales by running a knife around the edge. Invert onto serving plate or individual dinner plates. Makes 6 servings.

*Available at gourmet markets.

FRIED WILD RICE

8 dried shiitake mushrooms*
1 egg, beaten
2 tablespoons peanut oil
2 cups cooked wild rice, chilled
¾ cup diced cooked Chinese
    sausage*
½ cup peas, fresh or thawed frozen
1 yellow bell pepper, cored, seeded
    and cut in ¼-inch strips
2 green onions, cut in ½-inch diag-
    onal pieces
2 tablespoons Chicken Stock (page
    121)
1 tablespoon mushroom soy
    sauce*
Salt to taste

Soak dried mushrooms in hot water
to cover until softened, about 30
minutes. Drain; squeeze out excess moisture. Cut away and discard stems. Cut caps in small
pieces. Set aside. In a small skillet
cook beaten egg in 2 teaspoons
peanut oil (it will look like a pancake). Cool on paper towels. Cut in
strips and set aside. Heat wok over
high heat until smoking. Add remaining oil, swirling to coat sides of
pan; heat until smoking. Add
cooked rice and stir fry 1 to 2 minutes. Add reserved mushrooms,
Chinese sausage, peas, yellow bell
pepper, green onions, stock and
soy sauce; stir fry until heated
through, about 3 to 5 minutes. Remove from heat and add egg. Season with salt, if needed. Makes 6
servings.

*Available at oriental markets. Do
not substitute regular sausage for
the Chinese sausage.

WEDDING PILAF

1/3 cup small pieces of dried
vermicelli
4 tablespoons butter
2 tablespoons finely chopped onion
1 cup bulgur wheat
2 cups Chicken Stock (page 121)
Salt and freshly ground black pep-
    per to taste
2 tablespoons butter
½ cup chopped dried apricots
½ cup golden raisins
½ cup chopped almonds

In a large skillet cook vermicelli in
butter, stirring, until golden brown;
add onion and sauté 1 minute. Add
bulgur and stir to coat with butter.
Stir in chicken stock; season with
salt, if needed, and pepper. Cover,
bring to a boil, reduce heat and
cook 15 minutes. Transfer pilaf to
serving dish. In a medium skillet
melt the 2 tablespoons butter; stir in
dried fruits and nuts and heat
through. Arrange fruit mixture in an
attractive design on top of cooked
pilaf. Makes 4 servings.

HERBED ONION FOCCACIA

1 cup warm water (105°F.)
2 teaspoons dry yeast
3 to 3⅓ cups unbleached all-pur-
    pose flour
2 tablespoons minced fresh
    oregano
2 tablespoons minced fresh parsley
¼ cup freshly grated Parmesan
    cheese
1 teaspoon salt
2 medium onions, thinly sliced
3 tablespoons olive oil
2 garlic cloves, pressed
2 tablespoons freshly grated Par-
    mesan cheese
1 cup grated sharp Provolone
    cheese

Place water in large mixing bowl.
Sprinkle yeast over water and allow
to set 5 minutes until bubbly. Stir in
1 cup flour, oregano, parsley, ¼ cup
Parmesan cheese and salt; mix until smooth. Mix in enough remaining
flour to form a soft dough. Turn
dough out onto floured surface and
knead until smooth and elastic,
about 6 to 8 minutes. Place dough
in a lightly oiled medium bowl, turning to coat all sides with oil. Cover
with plastic wrap and place in warm
area (80 degrees) until doubled,
about 1 hour.

   In a medium skillet sauté onions
in 2 tablespoons olive oil until limp,
about 25 minutes; stir in garlic.
Grease jelly-roll pan. Punch dough

down. Turn out onto floured surface and roll into rectangle to fit pan. Transfer to prepared pan. Make indentations with finger over surface of dough. Sprinkle with remaining Parmesan cheese; spread onions on top. Drizzle with remaining olive oil. Let rise in warm area 35 to 40 minutes. Bake in a 450°F. oven 10 minutes; remove from oven and sprinkle with Provolone cheese. Return to oven and bake until golden brown, about 10 more minutes. Makes 1 large bread.

APPLE-PLUM SAUCE

2 pounds Golden Delicious apples (about 4 large), peeled, cored and cut in chunks
1 teaspoon fresh lemon juice
1 tablespoon sugar
1/3 cup water
1/2 cup bottled Chinese plum sauce*

In a medium saucepan combine apple chunks, lemon juice, sugar and water. Cook over medium heat until liquid begins to boil, reduce heat and simmer until apples are tender. Drain apples and cool to room temperature. Place the cooked apple chunks and plum sauce in food processor or blender and puree. Makes 6 servings.

*Available at oriental markets and well-stocked supermarkets.

CRANBERRY, ORANGE AND PEAR RELISH

1 large navel orange
1 pound (4 cups) fresh cranberries, washed and sorted
1/2 cup sugar
1/4 cup cranberry liqueur, or 1 tablespoon kirsch, or 2 tablespoons thawed frozen cranberry juice concentrate
3 pears, peeled, cored and quartered
1 tablespoon fresh lemon juice
8 fluted orange or lemon shells for serving containers (see Citrus Baskets, page 32)

Remove colored zest from the orange using a zester. Cut zest into 1/2-inch lengths; set aside. With a paring knife remove white membrane and discard. Section orange segments; set aside. In a food processor or blender combine cranberries and sugar using several on/off turns; process 5 seconds to mince berries. Transfer cranberries to glass mixing bowl and stir in liqueur. In a food processor or blender coarsely chop pear and orange segments using on/off turns; add to cranberries and lightly mix. Stir in lemon juice. Refrigerate until serving time. Serve in orange or lemon shells. Makes 8 servings.

GINGERED BAKED WINTER FRUITS

1 1/3 cups Muscat Canelli wine
1/3 cup brown sugar
1 teaspoon vanilla extract
1/2 teaspoon ground cinnamon
1/4 teaspoon ground allspice
1/4 teaspoon ground ginger
2 teaspoons finely chopped lemon zest (1 large or 2 small lemons)
3 tablespoons fresh lemon juice
1 pound dried apricots
1 pound dried peaches, cut in bite-sized pieces
4 tablespoons butter
1 cup chopped walnuts or pecans
1 tablespoon finely minced candied ginger

In a large bowl combine wine, sugar, vanilla, cinnamon, allspice, ginger, lemon zest and lemon juice. Combine apricots and peaches. Place half of the fruit in a greased 2-quart ovenproof casserole and dot with half of the butter which has been cut in small pieces. Add remaining fruit and dot with remaining butter. Spread nuts over the top of the fruit and cover with the wine mixture. Cover casserole and refrigerate for several hours or overnight. One hour before baking remove fruit from refrigerator. Bake in a 375°F. oven 45 minutes, stirring once or twice during baking time. Cool fruit and then stir in candied ginger. Makes 10 servings.

desserts

CHEESE-STUFFED NECTARINES

6 large firm, ripe nectarines
1 package (8 ounces) cream
   cheese, softened
2 tablespoons sugar
Pinch of salt
1 teaspoon almond extract
1 tablespoon kirsch or Amaretto
½ cup port

Remove the pits from the nectarines using the pitter or melon baller. Hollow-out the nectarine slightly to hold the cheese mixture. In a small bowl combine cream cheese, sugar, salt, almond extract and liqueur. Fill the nectarines with the cheese mixture; wrap in plastic wrap and chill until ready to serve. To serve, slice the nectarines crosswise with a fruit knife and arrange the slices on dessert plates. Pour 1 tablespoon port over each serving of nectarine slices. Makes 6 servings.

POACHED PEARS IN RED WINE

6 firm Bosc pears
½ cup sugar
1 bottle (750 ml) dry red wine (preferably a red zinfandel)
Strip of lemon peel
1 cinnamon stick (4-inch)
3 tablespoons pear brandy
Whipped cream or sorbet for accompaniment (optional)

Remove the peel from the pears; cut pears in half lengthwise. Remove cores with the melon baller. In a saucepan large enough to hold the pear halves combine the sugar, wine, lemon peel and cinnamon stick; bring to a boil and boil 5 minutes. Add the pear halves and poach 25 to 35 minutes, or until pears are tender (do not overcook; pears should be slightly firm). Cool pears in the syrup. Drain and return the syrup to the saucepan. Bring the syrup to a boil and cook over high heat for 10 minutes, or until syrup thickens. Cool syrup; stir in pear brandy. To serve, arrange pear halves on attractive dessert plates and garnish with whipped cream or serve with a scoop of sorbet. Makes 12 servings.

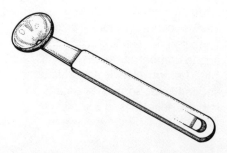

FRESH FRUIT CLAFOUTIS

1¼ pounds fresh fruit, halved and
  pitted (plums, nectarines,
  peaches or cherries)
3 tablespoons all-purpose flour
Pinch of salt
¼ cup sugar
4 eggs, at room temperature
2 cups milk
2 egg yolks, at room temperature
4 tablespoons brandy or kirsch
1 tablespoon confectioners' sugar

Butter a 9-inch quiche dish; place
the prepared fruit in dish. Sift the
flour with the salt and sugar into a
medium bowl. Gradually beat in 2
eggs, then the milk, then 2 eggs;
beat in egg yolks and brandy. Strain
the batter through a sieve over the
fruit. Bake in a 350°F. oven 45 minutes, or until the clafoutis is puffed
and brown. Serve warm (it will sink
slightly), sprinkled with confectioners' sugar. Makes 6 servings.

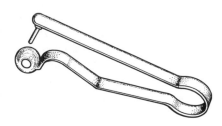

STRAWBERRY-PINEAPPLE AMBROSIA IN PINEAPPLE SHELLS

1 fresh pineapple
½ pint strawberries, washed and
  hulled
½ cup toasted almond slivers (page
  126)
3 tablespoons firmly packed brown
  sugar
¼ cup Grand Marnier or Cointreau
1 cup whipping cream
2 tablespoons toasted almond slivers for garnish (page 126)

Quarter the pineapple lengthwise.
With a grapefruit knife remove flesh
from each quarter and cut into 1-
inch cubes. Refrigerate pineapple
shells until serving time. In a large
bowl combine the pineapple
chunks, strawberries, almonds,
brown sugar and liqueur; chill 1
hour. In another large bowl, whip
cream and fold in fruit mixture; divide among the 4 pineapple shells.
Garnish each serving with almond
slivers. Makes 4 servings.

RASPBERRY-WINE SORBET

1 bottle (750 ml) zinfandel or dry
  premium red wine
½ cup sugar
2 tablespoons grated lemon peel
1 cinnamon stick (4-inch)
2 packages (10 ounces each) frozen raspberries in syrup
2 tablespoons fresh lemon juice
2 tablespoons raspberry liqueur

In a large saucepan combine wine,
2 cups water, sugar, lemon peel,
cinnamon stick and raspberries.
Bring to a boil, reduce heat and
simmer 5 minutes. Strain mixture
and cool to room temperature. Stir
in lemon juice and raspberry liqueur. Pour mixture into 2 shallow
metal pans and freeze at least 4
hours, or overnight. When ready to
serve, remove from freezer, soften
slightly and cut into chunks. Process in a blender or food processor
until smooth. Serve scoops of sorbet in sherbet dishes, stemmed
glasses or orange or lemon shells
(see Citrus Baskets, page 32).
Makes 8 servings.

TANGERINE SORBET WITH LYCHEES

½ cup sugar
1 can (6 ounces) frozen tangerine juice concentrate, thawed
¼ cup fresh lemon juice
2 tablespoons orange-flavored liqueur
1 can (15 ounces) peeled whole lychees, chilled
Fresh mint for garnish

In a medium saucepan combine 2 cups water and sugar. Cook, stirring constantly, over medium heat until mixture boils. Reduce heat and simmer 3 minutes; remove from heat and cool. Stir in the tangerine juice, lemon juice and liqueur. Pour into 2 square baking pans and freeze until firm, at least 4 hours, or overnight. To serve, drain lychees; spoon fruit into serving dishes. Remove sorbet from freezer, soften slightly and cut into chunks. Process in a blender or food processor until smooth. With ice cream scoop, form sorbet into balls, place on top of fruits and garnish with fresh mint; or, serve sorbet and lychees in orange shells (see Citrus Baskets, page 32) and garnish with mint. Makes 6 to 8 servings.

GINGERED NECTARINE, PEACH OR MANGO SORBET

½ cup dry white wine
⅓ cup sugar
2 tablespoons minced candied ginger
4 large ripe nectarines, peaches or mangoes, peeled, pitted and chopped
3 tablespoons fresh lemon juice
2 teaspoons grated lemon peel
1 pint strawberries, washed and hulled, for garnish

In a medium saucepan combine wine, sugar and ginger. Bring to a boil, reduce heat and simmer 5 minutes. Remove from heat, cool, then refrigerate until chilled. Combine chilled syrup, chopped fruit, lemon juice and lemon peel in a blender or food processor and puree. Pour into 2 square baking pans and freeze until firm, at least 4 hours, or overnight. When ready to serve, remove from freezer, soften slightly and cut into chunks. Process in a blender or food processor until smooth. Serve scoops of sorbet in sherbet dishes, stemmed glasses or lemon shells (see Citrus Baskets, page 32). Garnish with fresh strawberries. Makes 6 dessert or between-course servings.

COLD LEMON SOUFFLE

1 package unflavored gelatin
½ cup fresh lemon juice
4 eggs, separated and at room temperature
1½ cups sugar
3 tablespoons butter
⅛ teaspoon salt
Grated peel of 1 lemon
1 teaspoon vanilla extract
1 cup whipping cream
Long strips of lemon zest from 1 lemon, or chocolate curls (page 38) for garnish

Fit a 1-quart soufflé dish with a 6-inch band of waxed paper doubled and oiled to form a collar extending 2 inches above the rim; tie with a string around the outside of the dish.

Soften the gelatin in the lemon juice and set aside. In a double boiler beat the egg yolks; while beating, add 1 cup sugar, a small amount at a time, and beat until thick. Add lemon juice-gelatin mixture, butter and salt to the yolk mixture. Cook, stirring constantly, over hot, not boiling water, until thick, about 8 to 10 minutes. Remove from the heat and stir in lemon peel

and vanilla. Cool until mixture begins to stiffen; beat the egg whites until very soft peaks form. Add the remaining ½ cup sugar, a small amount at a time, and continue to beat until stiff peaks form. In a separate bowl, whip the cream until stiff. Fold the egg whites and whipped cream into the lemon mixture and turn into the prepared soufflé dish. Chill 4 hours before serving. Remove waxed paper collar. Garnish with strips of lemon zest or chocolate curls. Makes 6 servings.

FROZEN GRAND MARNIER SOUFFLE

1 cup sugar
2 tablespoons grated orange peel
6 egg yolks, at room temperature
¼ cup Grand Marnier
1 pint whipping cream
1 Pound Cake (page 128), cut in ½-inch cubes
Garnish: ½ cup heavy cream, whipped and flavored with 1 tablespoon Grand Marnier and 2 teaspoons sugar, and zest from 1 orange

Fit a 1-quart soufflé dish with a 6-inch band of waxed paper doubled and oiled to form a collar extending 2 inches above the rim; tie with a string around the outside of the dish.

In a small saucepan bring the sugar, ⅓ cup water and orange peel to a boil over medium-high heat. Cook the syrup to 220°F. on a candy thermometer. Beat the egg yolks until thick and lemon colored. Pour the syrup in a thin stream over the egg yolks and beat until thick; cool. Whisk the Grand Marnier into the egg yolk mixture. In a medium bowl whip 1 pint cream until stiff; fold into the egg yolk mixture. Spoon a 2-inch layer of the custard into the soufflé dish; top with half of the cake cubes. Cover with another layer of the custard mixture; add the remaining cake cubes. Spoon remaining custard mixture on top. Freeze 6 hours. To serve, remove waxed paper collar. Garnish with the flavored whipped cream and orange zest. Makes 6 servings.

KAHLUA MOUSSE

2 envelopes unflavored gelatin
½ cup sugar
⅛ teaspoon salt
¾ cup milk
1 package (6 ounces) semisweet chocolate chips
½ cup Kahlua
1 teaspoon vanilla extract
1½ cups whipping cream
Chocolate curls for garnish (page 38)

In a medium saucepan combine gelatin, sugar and salt. Stir in milk and chocolate chips; let sit 5 minutes. Cook over medium heat, stirring constantly, until gelatin is dissolved and chocolate is melted. Remove from heat and whisk until chocolate is well blended; stir in Kahlua and vanilla. Chill, stirring occasionally, until mixture mounds when dropped from a spoon (start checking at 30 minutes). Whip 1 cup whipping cream until stiff; fold into chilled chocolate mixture. Turn into 1-quart soufflé dish and chill until firm, about 4 hours. Just prior to serving, whip ½ cup whipping cream. Garnish top of mousse with whipped cream and chocolate curls. Makes 6 servings.

VARIATION For Kahlua Mousse Pie, prepare mousse and pour into Chocolate Crumb Crust (page 127). Garnish with whipped cream and chocolate curls.

ORANGE-CARAMEL FLAN

1 cup sugar
¼ cup water
2 navel oranges
2 cups milk
1 stick cinnamon (4-inch)
½ teaspoon vanilla extract
¼ teaspoon salt
3 eggs
1 egg yolk
½ cup sugar

For caramel: In small, heavy-bottomed saucepan or skillet bring the sugar and water to a boil over high heat, stirring until the sugar completely dissolves. Reduce heat to moderate and cook without stirring until the syrup turns a deep golden brown, at least 10 minutes. To do this in the microwave: Combine the sugar and water in a very deep, glass measuring cup. Microwave on high power 7 to 10 minutes (start checking at 7 minutes and keep checking every minute until syrup starts to turn a golden brown). Remove from microwave oven. Coat 6 custard cups with the caramel syrup. With a vegetable peeler remove the orange zest from the oranges; reserve. Remove the white membrane and discard. Divide orange sections among the custard cups; set cups aside while making the custard mixture.

For custard: In a medium saucepan bring the milk, orange peel and cinnamon stick to a boil over medium-high heat. Remove the pan from the heat, discard the orange peel and cinnamon stick; stir in the vanilla and the salt. In a medium bowl whisk the eggs and the egg yolk together until well-blended, then add the sugar gradually and continue to whisk. Whisk in the milk. Strain this mixture through a fine sieve into a pitcher or 1-quart measuring cup.

Divide the custard mixture among the caramel-lined custard cups. Place the custard cups in a large shallow baking pan. Pour enough boiling water into the pan to come halfway up the sides of the custard cups. Bake in a 350°F. oven 35 to 45 minutes, or until knife comes out clean when inserted in the center. Remove the custard cups and cool. Refrigerate. When ready to serve, unmold the custard by running a knife around the sides and place each custard cup in hot water briefly to soften caramel; invert onto individual dessert plates. Makes 6 servings.

PEACH MELBA MOUSSE PIE

2 cups finely crushed almond macaroon cookie crumbs*
6 tablespoons butter, melted
3 peaches, peeled, pitted and pureed (makes about 1 cup puree)
1 package (12 ounces) frozen whole raspberries (lightly sweetened—not in syrup), thawed, pureed and strained
2 tablespoons unflavored gelatin
3 tablespoons raspberry liqueur
2 tablespoons fresh lemon juice
⅓ cup sugar
¼ teaspoon almond extract
2 teaspoons grated lemon peel
3 egg whites, at room temperature
½ cup whipping cream
Fresh raspberries and sweetened whipped cream for garnish

Combine cookie crumbs and melted butter; press crumbs over the bottom and up the sides of a 10-inch springform pan. Bake in a 350°F. oven 6 minutes; set on a rack to cool.

In a large bowl combine the peach and raspberry purees; set aside. In a small saucepan, combine the gelatin, liqueur and lemon juice; soften 5 minutes. Dissolve gelatin over low heat; cool slightly. Add ⅓ cup sugar, cooled gelatin, almond extract and lemon peel to the pureed peach-raspberry mixture. Chill until mixture starts to set. In a large bowl beat egg whites until stiff, but not dry. Fold the chilled gelatin mixture into the egg whites. Whip the ½ cup whipping cream to soft peaks; fold into the peach-raspberry mixture. Pour into the prepared crust and chill until set. Just before serving, remove the sides of the springform pan; place the mousse on an attractive serving plate. Garnish with whipped cream and fresh raspberries. Makes 10 servings.

*Available at better French bakeries and gourmet markets.

COCONUT-ORANGE CHIFFON PIE

1¼ cups coconut macaroon cookie crumbs
2½ tablespoons melted butter
1¼ cups shredded coconut
1 envelope unflavored gelatin
½ cup sugar
¼ teaspoon salt
4 eggs, separated
¾ cup milk
½ cup orange juice
½ teaspoon vanilla extract
2 teaspoons grated orange peel (use peel from the 2 oranges that are to be sectioned for garnish)
½ cup whipping cream
2 medium oranges for garnish

For the crust: In a medium bowl combine the crumbs and butter. Press over bottom and sides of a 9-inch pie pan. Bake in a 350°F. oven 6 minutes; cool on rack.

Spread coconut in a shallow baking pan. Toast in a 350°F. oven, stirring frequently, until light brown. In a saucepan combine the gelatin, sugar and salt. Whisk in egg yolks. Gradually whisk in the milk and orange juice. Cook, stirring constantly, over medium heat until mixture simmers; remove from heat. Stir in vanilla and orange peel. Chill until mixture mounds slightly.

Beat the egg whites until stiff, but not dry, peaks form; fold into gelatin mixture. Whip cream until soft peaks form. Fold in whipped cream and ¾ cup toasted coconut. Pour into prepared pie shell. Refrigerate until firmly set, about 4 hours. Remove the white membrane from the two oranges and section fruit. Garnish pie with orange sections and remaining toasted coconut. Makes 6 to 8 servings.

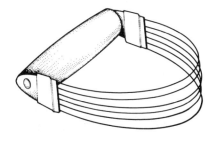

ALOHA APPLE PIE

1½ cups pineapple juice
¾ cup sugar
7 medium cooking apples, peeled, cored and cut in wedges
3 tablespoons cornstarch
1 tablespoon butter
½ teaspoon vanilla extract
½ teaspoon salt
1 baked 9-inch pastry shell (page 127)
½ pint whipping cream
½ cup chopped macadamia nuts

In a large saucepan bring 1¼ cups pineapple juice and sugar to a boil over medium-high heat; add apple wedges. Cover and simmer until apples are tender, but firm, about 3 to 4 minutes; remove from pan with slotted spoon. Combine cornstarch and remaining ¼ cup pineapple juice; add to syrup in saucepan. Cook, stirring, until thickened and bubbly. Remove from heat; add butter, vanilla and salt. Cool 10 minutes. Pour half of thickened pineapple sauce into baked shell, spreading evenly. Arrange cooked apples in shell; spoon remaining sauce over the top. Chill. When ready to serve whip the cream until stiff. Garnish pie with whipped cream and chopped nuts. Makes 8 servings.

NORMANDY APPLE TART

1 baked 10-inch Pâte Brisée shell
    (page 128)
1 jar (12 ounces) apricot jam
1 tablespoon brandy
8 cooking apples (Granny Smith or
    Rome Beauty)
½ cup sugar
Grated peel of 1 lemon
¼ pound unsalted butter
¼ cup Calvados
½ cup whipping cream
⅓ cup sugar
½ teaspoon ground cinnamon
¼ teaspoon freshly grated nutmeg
2 eggs
2 teaspoons vanilla extract
2 tablespoons sugar
⅓ cup sliced toasted almonds
1 cup Crème Fraîche (page 124) or
    1 cup whipping cream, whipped
    and flavored with 1 tablespoon
    Calvados and 2 tablespoons
    sugar for garnish

For glaze: In a small saucepan melt apricot jam; remove from heat and strain through a sieve into a bowl. Add brandy and whisk until smooth. Brush 2 tablespoons of the glaze on the baked tart shell.

For filling: Peel and core 6 of the apples and cut into ½-inch slices. In a large, heavy-bottomed skillet sauté apple slices, ½ cup sugar and lemon peel in butter until apples are slightly caramelized. Stir in Calvados and continue cooking another 1 to 2 minutes. Remove apple slices with a slotted spoon and let cool. Boil liquid until reduced to 3 tablespoons; set aside to cool.

For custard: In a small saucepan combine ½ cup cream, ⅓ cup sugar, cinnamon and nutmeg and heat for 1 minute. In a small bowl whisk eggs and gradually whisk in cream mixture. Add vanilla and reduced apple liquid.

Position rack in lower third of oven. Spread sautéed apples in tart shell. Peel remaining two apples, halve lengthwise and core each apple half with the melon baller. Cut the apple halves *crosswise* into thin slices. Arrange thin slices in a fan pattern over the cooked apples. Pour custard over apples to within ⅛ inch of the top. Bake tart in a 375°F. oven until apples are tender, about 30 to 40 minutes. Remove tart from oven (if using tart pan with removable sides, remove the outer ring). Heat broiler. Place tart pan on

a large cookie sheet. Sprinkle 2 tablespoons sugar over the top of the tart. Broil 6 to 8 inches from heat until top is caramelized (watch closely so top does not burn). Cool slightly on wire rack. Brush top of tart with the remaining apricot glaze and sprinkle with toasted almonds. Serve warm with crème fraîche or whipped cream. Makes 10 servings.

FRESH PLUM TART

1½ cups all-purpose flour
¼ teaspoon salt
6 tablespoons firmly packed brown
    sugar
¼ pound butter, softened
1 cup finely chopped almonds
2 tablespoons milk
7 fresh plums
¾ cup whipping cream
2 eggs
1 egg yolk
3 tablespoons Amaretto
¼ teaspoon almond extract
¼ cup sugar
¼ teaspoon salt
⅓ cup plum jam or currant jelly
⅓ cup sliced almonds
2 tablespoons sugar
½ pint vanilla ice cream or
    1 cup Crème Fraîche (page 124)
    for accompaniment

In a medium bowl combine flour, salt and brown sugar; blend in butter with pastry blender. With a fork, stir in the almonds and the milk. Press this mixture over the bottom and up the sides of a 9-inch tart pan (preferably one with a removable rim). Bake in a 375°F. oven 7 minutes. Remove to a wire rack.

Slice the plums in half, remove the pits and slice fruit crosswise into ¼-inch slices; arrange in baked tart shell. Combine cream, eggs and egg yolk, and whisk. Whisk in Amaretto, almond extract, ¼ cup sugar and salt. Pour custard mixture over plums. Bake tart in a 375°F. oven 45 to 50 minutes, or until plums are tender and custard is set; remove from oven (if using tart pan with removable sides, remove the outer ring). For glaze, melt jam in a small saucepan; brush over top of tart. Sprinkle with sliced almonds and sugar. Heat broiler. Place tart on a large cookie sheet. Broil 6 to 8 inches from heat until sugar is caramelized and nuts toasted (watch closely so top does not burn). Serve warm with a scoop of vanilla ice cream or a dollop of crème fraîche. Makes 8 servings.

ORANGE-GLAZED FRUIT TART

1 cup all-purpose flour
2 tablespoons confectioners' sugar
¼ pound butter or margarine
1 package (8 ounces) cream cheese, softened
¼ cup granulated sugar
3 tablespoons frozen orange juice concentrate, thawed
⅓ cup whipping cream
½ cup orange marmalade
Fresh fruits in season (1 pint strawberries, or 5 apricots and 4 plums)

In a medium bowl sift flour and confectioners' sugar together. With pastry blender cut in butter until mixture forms fine crumbs. Press dough over bottom and sides of a 9-inch tart pan. Bake in a 425°F. oven 8 to 10 minutes, or until lightly browned. Cool before filling.

With an electric mixer or food processor combine the cream cheese, sugar and orange juice concentrate. Gradually add the cream and beat until fluffy. Spread in cooled, baked tart shell; chill. Heat the marmalade. Strain and cool to lukewarm. Slice the fruit. Arrange fruit in an attractive design on the filling; brush with marmalade. Make 8 servings.

HARVEST PEAR PIE

1 unbaked 9-inch pastry shell (page 127)
7 firm, ripe Bartlett pears, peeled, cored (see Note) and sliced
½ cup sugar
3 tablespoons fresh lemon juice
1 teaspoon grated lemon peel
½ cup sugar
½ cup all-purpose flour
½ teaspoon ground ginger
½ teaspoon ground cinnamon
¼ teaspoon ground mace
6 tablespoons butter
½ pint whipping cream
2 tablespoons sugar
½ teaspoon vanilla extract

In a large mixing bowl combine sliced pears, ½ cup sugar, lemon juice and lemon peel. Place mixture in pastry shell. In a medium bowl combine ½ cup sugar with flour and spices. With pastry blender cut butter into dry ingredients until crumbly. Top pears with crumb mixture. Bake in a 400°F. oven 45 minutes. Whip cream until stiff; add sugar and vanilla. Serve pie warm with whipped cream. Makes 8 servings.

NOTE Use a melon baller to core pears.

PEAR OR NECTARINE CRISP

6 firm, ripe pears or nectarines
¾ cup sugar
½ teaspoon ground cinnamon
¼ teaspoon ground cloves
1 tablespoon fresh lemon juice
¾ cup all-purpose flour
⅛ teaspoon salt
6 tablespoons butter
½ cup chopped pecans
Calvados ice cream (1 pint good
    quality vanilla ice cream, soft-
    ened and flavored with 2 to 3
    tablespoons Calvados)

If using pears, peel and core (see
Note). Slice fruit and place in a
large bowl. Add ½ cup sugar,
spices and lemon juice. Mix lightly
and pour into a buttered 1½-quart
baking dish. In a medium bowl
combine remaining ¼ cup sugar,
flour, salt and butter to a crumbly
consistency. Add the nuts. Sprinkle
over the fruit. Bake in a 350°F. oven
45 minutes, or until the fruit is tender and the crust is nicely browned.
Serve with Calvados ice cream.
Makes 6 to 8 servings.

NOTE Use a melon baller to core
the pears. Nectarines make this a
special dessert in the summertime.
The recipe was developed after a
two-week trip to the wine country of
Napa, Sonoma and Mendocino in
northern California.

APRICOT STRUDEL

1 package (6 ounces) dried apri-
    cots, cut in ¼-inch strips
1 cup apricot nectar
½ cup sugar
1 cup chopped walnuts
Zest from 1 lemon, cut fine
1 tablespoon fresh lemon juice
⅔ cup finely grated tart green apple
    (1 large)
¼ teaspoon almond extract
6 sheets filo dough
¼ pound unsalted butter, melted
½ cup dry white bread crumbs
    (preferably homemade, page
    126)
1 tablespoon confectioners' sugar

In a medium saucepan bring apricot strips, apricot nectar and sugar
to a boil. Reduce heat and simmer
until the apricots are completely
soft and most of the liquid is absorbed, 10 to 12 minutes. Remove
from heat and cool slightly. Stir in
the nuts, lemon zest, lemon juice,
grated apple and almond extract.
Taste and add more sugar, if
needed. To prepare filo: Refer to
Shaping and Forming Strudels
(page 42). Use melted butter and
bread crumbs between filo layers.
Bake apricot strudel in a 400°F.
oven 20 to 30 minutes (remove

from oven after 10 minutes and pre-
cut slices nearly through). When
strudel is nicely browned, remove
to a cooling rack. When cool, dust
with confectioners' sugar. Makes 1
strudel, 8 to 10 servings.

PEAR, GORGONZOLA AND WALNUT FILO TORTE

3½ cups dry red wine
1¼ cups sugar
1 piece vanilla bean (2-inch), split
⅛ teaspoon white pepper
Zest from 1 large lemon, cut in ¾-
    inch lengths
5 firm, ripe pears, peeled, halved
    and cored (see Note)
1 package (3 ounces) cream
    cheese, at room temperature
2 ounces Gorgonzola cheese, at
    room temperature
½ cup chopped walnuts
8 sheets filo dough
½ pound unsalted butter, melted
¼ cup ground walnuts combined
    with 2 tablespoons sugar
Sweetened whipped cream fla-
    vored with pear brandy or kirsch
    (optional)

In a large, heavy-bottomed saucepan heat the wine, sugar, vanilla
bean, pepper and lemon zest. Add
pear halves and simmer 10 minutes
(pears will still be firm). Let pears
cool in wine syrup. When cool re-

move pears from syrup. Strain wine mixture; return to saucepan. Boil over high heat until reduced to ¾ cup, 15 to 20 minutes. Remove from heat and cool to room temperature.

In a blender, food processor or with an electric mixer combine cheeses and walnuts. Fill each pear half with cheese mixture. Brush each sheet of filo, one at a time, with melted butter. Sprinkle 1 teaspoon of the walnut-sugar mixture over ½ of each sheet. Fold filo in half and brush again with melted butter. Place filo, buttered side down, in 12-inch shallow tart pan. Repeat using 6 more of the sheets; arrange in a pinwheel in the tart pan, with leaves extending over the sides of the pan. Butter the last sheet and fold in half. Place over the first leaves to completely seal bottom. Butter the layered filo and sprinkle any remaining walnut-sugar mixture over the bottom. Arrange pear halves radiating from center. Fold and roll extended filo leaves to form a 2 inch rim of crust; brush with melted butter. Bake torte in a 375°F. oven 20 to 25 minutes, or until crust is golden brown. Serve with flavored whipped cream, if desired. Pour wine syrup into pitcher and serve with torte. Makes 8 servings.

NOTE Use a melon baller to core pears.

ZUCCHINI BUNDT CAKE

3 eggs
2 cups sugar
1 cup vegetable oil
1 teaspoon vanilla extract
1 teaspoon ground cinnamon
1 teaspoon salt
1 teaspoon baking soda
¼ teaspoon baking powder
1 package (8 ounces) cream cheese, softened
3 cups all-purpose flour
2 cups grated zucchini
2 cups chopped walnuts
1 tablespoon confectioners' sugar

In a large bowl beat eggs, sugar, oil, vanilla, cinnamon, salt, baking soda, baking powder and cream cheese until well mixed. Add flour and mix until well blended. Fold in grated zucchini and nuts. Turn into a greased and floured bundt pan. Bake in a 325°F. oven 1 hour, or until toothpick inserted comes out clean. Cool in pan on rack 10 minutes, then turn out onto rack to finish cooling. When cool, dust with confectioners' sugar. Makes 12 to 16 servings.

NOTE This moist cake keeps well and can be frozen.

FRESH APPLE CAKE

2 eggs
2 cups sugar
1 cup vegetable oil
4 cups grated apples (Rome, McIntosh or Golden Delicious)
2½ cups all-purpose flour
1 teaspoon salt
2 teaspoons ground cinnamon
2 teaspoons baking soda
1 cup chopped walnuts
¼ cup sugar
2 tablespoons Calvados

In a large bowl beat the eggs for 2 minutes; add the sugar and oil and mix well. Stir in the grated apples and let stand 20 minutes. Sift together the flour, salt, cinnamon and baking soda; add to the apple mixture. Stir in the chopped nuts. Pour batter into a greased and floured tube pan or bundt pan; bake in a 350°F. 1 hour, or until toothpick inserted comes out clean. Combine ½ cup water and sugar in a small saucepan; bring to a boil. Reduce heat and simmer 3 minutes. Remove from heat and stir in Calvados. Cool cake in pan on rack 10 minutes; then turn out onto rack to finish cooling. Poke holes in the cake with a toothpick; slowly pour the Calvados glaze over the cake. Makes 12 to 16 servings.

PERSIMMON CAKE

2 cups sugar
2 tablespoons butter
2 cups persimmon pulp
3 cups all-purpose flour
3 teaspoons baking soda
1 teaspoon salt
1 teaspoon ground cinnamon
½ teaspoon freshly grated nutmeg
½ teaspoon ground cloves
1 cup milk
2 cups chopped walnuts
2 cups raisins dusted with 1 table-
    spoon all-purpose flour

In a large bowl cream together the sugar and butter. Add the persimmon pulp and mix well. Sift together the flour, baking soda, salt and spices. Add the dry ingredients alternately with the milk to the persimmon mixture. Stir in the walnuts and the raisins. Pour cake batter into a well-greased and floured 9-by 5-inch loaf pan. Bake in a 325°F. oven 90 minutes. Makes 8 to 10 servings.

NOTE Persimmons are ready to use when they become soft; halve and scoop out the pulp.

PUMPKIN RING

2½ cups all-purpose flour
2 cups sugar
2 teaspoons ground cinnamon
1 teaspoon salt
½ teaspoon baking powder
½ teaspoon baking soda
½ teaspoon ground ginger
½ teaspoon freshly grated nutmeg
½ cup margarine, softened
1 cup mashed pumpkin
2 eggs
1 cup chopped walnuts
1 cup confectioners' sugar
2 tablespoons fresh lemon juice
½ teaspoon grated lemon peel

Into large mixing bowl sift dry ingredients. Add margarine, ½ cup water and pumpkin. Beat 2 minutes with an electric mixer on medium speed; scrape sides and bottom of bowl. Add eggs and beat an additional 2 minutes; stir in walnuts. Pour into a greased and floured bundt pan. Bake in a 350°F. oven 50 to 60 minutes, or until toothpick inserted comes out clean. Cool in pan on rack 10 minutes, then turn out onto rack to finish cooling. Combine confectioners' sugar, lemon juice and lemon peel; stir. When cake has cooled, pour over the top and the sides. Makes 12 to 16 servings.

ALMOND CAKE WITH RASPBERRY SAUCE

¾ cup sugar
¼ pound unsalted butter, at room
    temperature
1 package (7 ounces) almond
    paste
3 eggs, at room temperature
1 tablespoon kirsch or triple sec
¼ teaspoon almond extract
¾ cup all-purpose flour
½ teaspoon baking powder
1 tablespoon confectioners' sugar
1 package (12 ounces) frozen rasp-
    berries (lightly sweetened—not
    in syrup), thawed, pureed and
    strained
2 tablespoons kirsch or raspberry
    liqueur

In a large bowl combine sugar, butter and almond paste; beat until well mixed. Add eggs, one at a time, beating well after each addition. Add liqueur and almond extract. Sift flour and baking powder over mixture and fold in (do not overmix). Turn into greased and floured 8-inch round cake pan. Bake in a 350°F. oven about 40 to 50 minutes, or until toothpick inserted in center comes out clean.

Cool and dust lightly with confectioners' sugar. Combine raspberry puree with liqueur. To serve, slice cake and place on individual dessert plates. Top with raspberry sauce. Place any additional sauce in attractive pitcher and serve. Makes 8 to 10 servings.

NOTE This almond cake is a nice finish to a Chinese dinner.

SPICED CHOCOLATE LOAF

¼ pound butter
1 cup sugar
2 eggs
1¾ cups sifted all-purpose flour
1 teaspoon baking soda
½ teaspoon salt
1 teaspoon ground cinnamon
½ teaspoon freshly grated nutmeg
    or ground mace
¼ teaspoon ground cloves
¼ teaspoon ground ginger
¾ cup canned pumpkin
¾ cup semisweet chocolate chips
¾ cup chopped walnuts
Spicy Glaze (following)

In a large bowl cream butter with an electric mixer. Add sugar gradually, beating until fluffy. Add eggs and beat well. Sift the dry ingredients together; add to creamed mixture alternately with pumpkin, beginning and ending with dry ingredients. Fold in the chocolate chips and ½ cup of the nuts; pour batter into greased and floured 9- by 5-inch loaf pan. Sprinkle top with the remaining walnuts. Bake in a 350°F. oven 55 minutes. Cool on rack for 10 minutes, and then remove from pan. Drizzle with Spicy Glaze. Makes 8 to 10 servings.

SPICY GLAZE In a small bowl combine ½ cup sifted confectioners' sugar, ⅛ teaspoon ground cinnamon, ⅛ teaspoon freshly grated nutmeg, 2 tablespoons softened butter and 1 tablespoon whipping cream.

HAZELNUT MERINGUE BLOSSOM PARFAITS

3 egg whites at room temperature
¼ teaspoon cream of tartar
⅛ teaspoon salt
¾ cup sugar
¼ cup finely ground toasted hazelnuts (page 126)
Crème Anglaise (page 125)
2 cups assorted fresh fruits in season (peaches or nectarines, raspberries and blueberries)
Sauce aux Framboise (page 125)

In a medium bowl beat egg whites with cream of tartar and salt with an electric mixer on high speed until very soft peaks form. Add ½ cup sugar slowly and continue beating until stiff and glossy. Mix remaining ¼ cup sugar and hazelnuts together. Carefully fold nut mixture into meringue with a rubber spatula (use as few motions as possible—too much folding will decrease the volume of the meringue). Place meringue mixture in pastry bag fitted with large star tube and pipe out 2-inch cookie-shaped meringues onto 3 parchment-lined cookie sheets; or, use two teaspoons to form the meringues. Bake in a 275°F. oven 1½ hours. Turn oven off and leave meringues in oven for several hours or overnight to dry out.

To serve, place 2 tablespoons Crème Anglaise in 6 stemmed glasses, then a meringue blossom, then assorted fresh fruits and additional Crème Anglaise; drizzle Sauce aux Framboise over all. Makes 6 servings.

NOTE There will be extra meringue blossoms; store in a cool dry place for future use, or serve as cookies.

CHESTNUT MOUSSE CAKE

Genoise:
4 tablespoons butter
4 eggs, separated and at room
  temperature
2/3 cup plus 2 tablespoons sugar
1 teaspoon vanilla extract
Pinch of salt
1 1/4 cups sifted cake flour

Mousse:
4 eggs plus 3 egg yolks, at room
  temperature
1/2 cup sugar
2 tablespoons unflavored gelatin
1/4 cup dark rum
2 cups sweetened canned chestnut
  puree
1 tablespoon grated orange peel
1 cup whipping cream

Buttercream Frosting:
6 ounces semisweet chocolate, cut
  in small pieces
3 tablespoons strong coffee
1/4 pound plus 4 tablespoons unsalted butter, cut in 8 pieces and
  at room temperature
Chocolate leaves (page 37) and
  orange peel rose (page 34) for
  garnish

For genoise: Butter a 9-inch round cake pan, line with waxed paper, and butter and flour the paper. Melt the 4 tablespoons butter; cool. In a large mixing bowl beat the egg yolks until they are lemon-colored; slowly beat in the 2/3 cup sugar and continue to beat for 8 minutes, or until thick and pale yellow. Add the vanilla extract. Beat the egg whites and salt until stiff, but not dry. Add the remaining 2 tablespoons sugar and beat until whites are glossy. Fold one-third of the egg whites into the yolk mixture. Blend in one-third of the flour, then one-third egg whites, then repeat until all flour and egg white is incorporated. Gently fold in the melted butter (do not overmix—keep the batter light). Spoon into prepared cake pan and bake in a 350°F. oven until cake has puffed and pulled slightly from the edges of the pan, 25 to 30 minutes; cool in the pan on a rack.

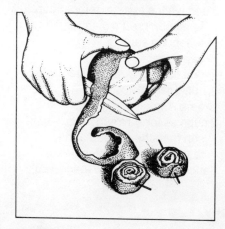

For chestnut mousse: In a large mixing bowl beat the 4 eggs, 3 egg yolks and sugar together. In a small saucepan combine gelatin, rum and 1/4 cup water. Let gelatin soften; dissolve the gelatin over low heat. Cool. Combine the chestnut puree with the egg mixture. Add the cooled gelatin and the grated orange peel. In a large bowl whip the cream until stiff. Fold gently into the chestnut mixture.

To form the mousse cake: Line a 6-cup bowl with plastic wrap. Let plastic wrap drape over sides. Remove the genoise from the cake pan. With a serrated knife cut the genoise into 3 thin layers. Cut 2 of the layers into wedges; use to completely line bowl. Press the cake to the sides of the bowl. Spoon the mousse into the lined bowl; fill to the very top. Cover the top with the uncut layer of cake, cutting to fit if larger than bowl. Bring the plastic wrap up and over to cover the cake completely; refrigerate overnight.

For buttercream frosting: In a small, heavy-bottomed saucepan melt chocolate with coffee over low heat. Remove pan from heat and beat in butter, one piece at a time, until mixture is smooth. Chill frosting until mixture thickens to a spreading consistency. Remove mousse cake from bowl and peel off plastic wrap. Invert cake onto a serving plate. Frost with butter-cream. Refrigerate up to two days.

To serve, remove cake from refrigerator about 20 minutes prior to serving to allow buttercream to soften. Garnish with chocolate leaves and orange peel rose. Serves 10 to 12.

NOTE This is a lengthy recipe consisting of genoise, mousse and buttercream frosting. It is a spectacular dessert worth every minute of preparation time. The advantage of this dessert is that it should be made two days ahead to allow flavors to fully develop. The genoise can be made several weeks ahead and frozen.

CHOCOLATE ECLAIR TORTE

½ cup chopped walnuts
2 tablespoons sugar
¼ pound butter, cut into 6 pieces
1 cup sifted all-purpose flour
¼ teaspoon salt
4 eggs, at room temperature
¾ cup sugar
3 tablespoons cornstarch
¼ teaspoon salt
2½ cups milk
3 eggs, at room temperature
2 teaspoons vanilla extract
6 tablespoons confectioners' sugar
4 tablespoons butter, softened
4 ounces semisweet chocolate
3 tablespoons butter
½ cup whipping cream

For pastry: Mix walnuts and sugar; set aside. In a medium saucepan combine 1 cup water and butter; bring to a rolling boil. Reduce heat to medium, add flour and salt all at once, stirring until dough forms a ball and looks like cornmeal mush. Remove from heat and cool 2 minutes. Add eggs, one at a time, beating well after each addition (mixture should lose its sheen when eggs are thoroughly incorporated). Lightly grease three 9-inch round cake pans with removable sides. Divide dough evenly among the three pans; spread to sides. Sprinkle with sugar-nut mixture. Bake in a 400°F. oven 15 minutes. Open oven and press dough down with a spatula. Reduce oven temperature to 375°F. and bake until dough is lightly browned, about 15 minutes. Turn off heat, open door slightly and let pastry stand 10 minutes. Remove from oven. Remove sides of cake pans. With long spatula loosen and remove pastry from pan bottoms and set on racks to cool.

For custard: In a medium, heavy-bottomed saucepan combine sugar, cornstarch and salt. Whisk in milk and eggs until thoroughly combined. Bring to a boil over medium-high heat, whisking constantly until thickened, about 5 minutes. Immediately set pan in sink partially filled with cold water and ice cubes and stir custard until cool; add vanilla. In a medium bowl beat confectioners' sugar and butter until smooth. Add custard, a few tablespoons at a time, and beat until thoroughly mixed.

For glaze: In a small, heavy-bottomed saucepan melt chocolate and butter together over low heat; stir to combine. Working quickly, drizzle glaze over each layer of pastry.

To assemble: Place one pastry layer, chocolate side up, on a serving plate. Place half of custard in center and spread with spatula to the edges. Add second layer, chocolate side up. Spread with remaining custard and add last pastry layer; chill thoroughly. Just before serving, whip cream until stiff; place in pastry bag and pipe around top and sides of torte. Use a serrated knife and a sawing motion to cut the torte. Makes 10 servings.

CHOCOLATE CURRANT AMARETTO CHEESECAKE

2½ cups finely crushed chocolate cookie crumbs
½ cup chopped toasted almonds (page 126)
¼ pound butter, melted
½ cup dried currants
⅓ cup Amaretto
3 packages (8 ounces each) cream cheese, softened
¾ cup sugar
4 eggs
1 package (6 ounces) chocolate chips, melted and cooled
1 cup sour cream
4 tablespoons butter, melted
1 teaspoon vanilla extract
1 tablespoon grated orange peel
1 cup sour cream
2 tablespoons Amaretto
½ cup toasted sliced almonds for garnish (page 126)

In a medium bowl combine crushed cookie crumbs and chopped toasted almonds. Stir in melted butter and press mixture firmly on bottom and 2 inches up sides of a 10-inch springform pan. Bake in a 350°F. oven 6 minutes; cool. Soak currants in the Amaretto until plump; drain and reserve liquid. In a food processor blend cream cheese and sugar. Add eggs, one at a time, and process until smooth. Blend in melted chocolate chips, 1 cup sour cream, liqueur from currants, melted butter and vanilla; stir in the orange peel and currants. Pour into prepared crust. Bake in a 350°F. oven 1 hour, or until set. Stir together remaining sour cream and 2 tablespoons Amaretto. Spread over the top of the cheesecake. Return to a 350°F. oven and bake 3 minutes. Cool, then cover and chill. To serve, slice and garnish each serving with toasted sliced almonds. Makes 12 servings.

BING CHERRY CHEESECAKE

1⅔ cups graham cracker crumbs
4 tablespoons butter, melted
2 tablespoons sugar (optional)
2 packages (8 ounces each) cream cheese, softened
½ cup sugar
4 eggs
1 teaspoon grated lemon peel
1 teaspoon vanilla extract
½ cup cherry preserves or currant jelly
2 tablespoons cherry liqueur
½ pound fresh bing cherries, pitted

In a medium bowl combine crumbs, melted butter and sugar, if desired. Press crumbs on the bottom and 1 inch up the sides of a 9-inch springform pan. Bake in a 350°F. oven 5 minutes; cool on rack. In a large mixing bowl with an electric mixer (or in a food processor) beat cream cheese and sugar. Add eggs, one at a time, beating well after each addition. Add lemon peel and vanilla and mix thoroughly. Turn mixture into prepared crust and bake in a 350°F. oven 50 to 60 minutes, or until set. Cool and chill.

In a small saucepan melt cherry preserves over low heat. Remove from heat; add liqueur and cherries. Cool. Just prior to serving, remove sides from springform pan. Place a slice of cheesecake on individual dessert plates and spoon cherry topping over each slice. Makes 10 servings.

Photograph: Normandy Apple Tart.

CHICKEN STOCK

5 pounds assorted chicken parts
(necks, wings, backs)
2 leeks
1 large onion, quartered
2 large carrots
5 sprigs fresh parsley
2 stalks celery, including leaves
6 peppercorns, crushed
1 teaspoon salt

In a large stock pot place chicken parts. Cover with 3 quarts cold water and bring to a boil; skim off scum from the surface. Add the leeks, onion, carrots, parsley, celery, peppercorns and salt. Simmer, partially covered, 2½ to 3 hours. Remove the chicken and reserve for another use. Strain the stock through a colander or sieve lined with a double thickness of dampened cheesecloth. Refrigerate overnight. Remove the hardened fat on the surface. Makes 2½ quarts.

NOTE For extra-rich stock, boil and reduce the stock to 1½ quarts. Use the extra rich stock for velouté sauce and soup.

FISH STOCK

2 pounds lean fresh fish trimmings,
including bones (do not include
trimmings from salmon)
1 onion, thinly sliced
2 carrots, cut in chunks
6 fresh parsley sprigs
1 stalk celery
2 lemon slices
½ teaspoon salt
1 bay leaf
8 peppercorns
1 cup dry white wine

In large stainless steel or enamel stock pot combine all ingredients and 2½ quarts water. Bring to a simmer, skim, then simmer, uncovered, 30 minutes. Remove from heat and strain through a strainer lined with a double thickness of dampened cheesecloth. Makes 2 quarts.

NOTE Fish stock may be refrigerated up to 2 days and frozen up to 3 months. When using fish stock that has been frozen, boil 5 minutes before using.

Photograph: Red cabbage filled with Spinach-Basil Pesto, in basket of assorted crudités and cooked tortellini.

BEEF STOCK

3 pounds beef shin
2 marrow bones
3 pounds beef chuck, cut in 3
  pieces
1 large onion
1 large or 2 small leeks, rinsed well
2 carrots
2 sprigs fresh parsley
2 stalks celery
1 turnip
2 teaspoons salt
6 peppercorns
1 bay leaf
½ teaspoon thyme

Remove the meat from the shinbone and reserve. In a large saucepan place the shinbone and marrow bones in boiling water. Cook 5
minutes; drain. Place the bones
and all meat in a large stock pot.
Add 3½ quarts water. Bring to a
rolling boil and reduce heat; skim
off scum from surface (continue to
skim throughout cooking process).
Add the onion, leek, carrots, parsley, celery, turnip and salt. Tie peppercorns, bay leaf and thyme in
cheesecloth bag and add. Simmer
over low heat 4 to 5 hours. Remove
the meat and reserve for another
use. Strain liquid through a colander or sieve lined with a double
thickness of dampened cheesecloth. If a richer flavor is desired,
continue to simmer until desired flavor is reached. Season with additional salt if needed. Makes 3
quarts.

NOTE Prepare Glace de Viande by
reducing stock down to ½ cup. Use
a total of ½ teaspoon salt; taste
near the end of the reduction and
add additional salt if needed.

DUCK STOCK

1 duck (4 to 5 pounds)
2 tablespoons Shaosing wine*
4 slices (⅛ inch thick) fresh ginger
  root
4 green onions, including tops
½ teaspoon salt

Remove the giblets from the duck.
Rinse the duck and pat dry. Prick
the duck all over with a meat fork.
Place duck on a rack in a roasting
pan; roast in a 375°F. oven 60 to 75
minutes, or until skin is golden
brown and breast meat is slightly
pink. Cool. Pour off accumulated
fat; reserve the duck drippings in
roasting pan. Carefully carve and
remove the duck breasts; reserve
for another recipe. Carve duck legs,
remove duck meat and cut into fine
slivers (use in Duck Leg Soup,
page 59). In a large stock pot combine the carved duck carcass, the
giblets, 6 cups water, Shaosing
wine, ginger slices, green onions
and salt; bring to a boil over high
heat. Reduce heat to low and simmer, covered, for 1½ hours.

Take 1 cup of the stock and pour
into roasting pan. Scrape and stir
up duck drippings, and combine
with remaining stock. Remove duck
carcass and giblets from stock;
strain stock through a strainer lined
with two thicknesses of dampened
cheesecloth. Cool stock; chill.
When stock has thoroughly chilled,
remove the hardened fat and discard. Makes 1½ quarts.

NOTE Any duck meat on carcass
may be removed and slivered for
use in soup. Giblets may also be
diced and used in soup if desired.
Stock can be stored in the refrigerator up to 3 days or frozen for 2
months.

*Available at oriental markets.

COURT BOUILLON

2 bottles (8 ounces each) clam
  juice
1 cup dry white wine
1 lemon, thinly sliced
1 stalk celery including leaves, cut
  in 2-inch pieces
½ onion, sliced
1 carrot, cut in 2-inch pieces
3 sprigs fresh parsley

In a large saucepan bring the clam juice, 2 cups water, wine, lemon and vegetables to a boil; reduce heat and simmer, uncovered, until the liquid has been reduced to 3 cups, about 25 minutes. Strain through a strainer lined with a double thickness of dampened cheesecloth. Makes 3 cups.

NOTE Court Bouillon may be frozen for up to 3 months.

BEARNAISE SAUCE

4 egg yolks
6 tablespoons fresh lemon juice
½ pound butter, cut in 16 pieces
    and chilled
2 tablespoons finely minced fresh
    parsley
1 tablespoon minced fresh tarragon
    or 1 teaspoon crushed dried
    tarragon
2 tablespoons tarragon vinegar

In a small, heavy-bottomed saucepan whisk egg yolks and lemon juice; add half of butter. Cook over very low heat, whisking until butter is melted. Add remaining butter. Continue whisking until butter is melted and sauce is thickened, about 6 to 8 minutes. Add the parsley, tarragon and vinegar. Keep warm in a small thermos or place in a double boiler over hot, not simmering or boiling, water. Makes ¾ cup.

ENRICHED BECHAMEL SAUCE

2 shallots, minced
3 tablespoons butter
5 tablespoons all-purpose flour
1 cup milk, at room temperature
4 egg yolks
Salt and white pepper to taste

In a medium, heavy-bottomed saucepan sauté the shallots in butter until golden. Blend in the flour, stirring well. Cook until bubbly. Remove from the heat and whisk in the milk. Return to heat and cook over low heat, whisking frequently, until the sauce thickens, about 3 minutes; remove from heat. Whisk the egg yolks. Whisk in a small amount of the sauce, then return the egg yolk mixture to the sauce. Heat 2 minutes, whisking constantly. Season with salt and pepper. Makes 1¼ cups.

SAUCE JOINVILLE

½ cup butter
½ cup flour
2 cups Court Bouillon (page 122)
⅔ cup half-and-half, at room
    temperature
4 egg yolks
¼ cup dry sherry
¼ cup whipping cream
1 tablespoon tomato paste
Salt and freshly ground black pep-
    per to taste

In a medium saucepan melt the butter. Stir in the flour and cook until the mixture foams and is golden. Whisk in the court bouillon and continue to whisk until the mixture is smooth. Cook until slightly thickened, stirring constantly. Whisk in the half-and-half and simmer 2 minutes.

In a small bowl whisk the yolks, dry sherry and cream. Whisk a small amount of the sauce into the yolk mixture, then add this to the remaining sauce in the saucepan. Cook over low heat 2 minutes, stirring constantly. Add tomato paste and whisk well. Season with salt and pepper. Makes approximately 3 cups.

SALSA SUPREME

5 large fresh tomatoes, peeled, seeded and chopped
1 small red onion, chopped
2 cloves garlic, pressed
1 tablespoon seeded, finely minced fresh jalapeño peppers
2 to 3 tablespoons chopped fresh cilantro
2 teaspoons fresh lemon or lime juice
1 teaspoon salt

In a large bowl combine all ingredients and mix well. Cover and refrigerate.

NOTE Hotness of salsa will depend on amount of jalapeño pepper added. Increase or decrease according to personal taste. Garlic may also be increased if desired. Wear rubber gloves when working with fresh chile peppers.

FRENCH VINAIGRETTE

½ cup safflower oil
2 tablespoons olive oil
3 tablespoons fresh lemon juice
1 tablespoon grated onion
¾ teaspoon dry mustard
½ teaspoon celery salt
¼ teaspoon white pepper
2 teaspoons fresh tarragon or ½ teaspoon crushed dried tarragon
½ teaspoon coarse salt
1 clove garlic, minced fine or pressed
1 teaspoon sugar

In a small bowl whisk together all ingredients. Makes ¾ cup.

NOTE This is a wonderful all-purpose French dressing to have on hand all the time. It is a perfect marinade for mushrooms and other fresh vegetables.

CREAMY FRENCH DRESSING

¼ cup tarragon vinegar
2 teaspoons fresh lemon juice
1 egg, lightly beaten
½ cup whipping cream
3 tablespoons olive oil
½ cup safflower oil
1 clove garlic, pressed
1 teaspoon Dijon-style mustard
½ teaspoon Worcestershire sauce
½ teaspoon sugar
¼ teaspoon salt
¼ teaspoon white pepper

In a medium bowl whisk together all ingredients. Chill thoroughly and whisk again just before using. Makes 1½ cups.

TART FRENCH DRESSING

½ cup safflower oil
2 tablespoons catsup
2 tablespoons fresh lemon juice or white wine vinegar
3 tablespoons fresh orange juice
½ teaspoon dry mustard
¼ teaspoon paprika
¼ teaspoon salt

In a small bowl whisk together all ingredients. Makes 1 cup.

CREME FRAICHE

1 cup whipping cream (not ultrapasteurized)
2 tablespoons buttermilk

In a small bowl whisk the buttermilk into the whipping cream until thoroughly blended. In a small, heavy-bottomed saucepan heat mixture until just slightly warm (85 degrees). Place cream mixture in glass jar with loose-fitting lid. Keep in warm place (at least 60 degrees, but not over 85 degrees), until cream thickens. Makes 1 cup.

CREME PATISSIERE

1½ cups milk
½ cup sugar
4 egg yolks
¼ cup all-purpose flour
½ teaspoon vanilla extract

In a small, heavy-bottomed sauce-pan scald milk over medium-high heat; set aside. In a medium bowl whisk the sugar and egg yolks together until creamy and smooth. Add the flour and whisk until smooth. Slowly whisk in the scalded milk. Return to saucepan and bring just to a boil over medium-high heat, whisking constantly (do not let the mixture boil). Remove from the heat and cool. Stir in the vanilla. Makes 2½ cups.

CREME ANGLAISE

3 egg yolks
⅓ cup granulated sugar
1¼ cups hot milk
2 teaspoons vanilla extract
1 to 2 tablespoons rum
1 tablespoon softened butter

In a heavy-bottomed saucepan whisk the egg yolks until lemon-colored; gradually whisk in the sugar, then whisk in the milk. Cook over low heat, whisking constantly, until sauce thickens enough to coat a metal spoon (do not let the sauce simmer or it will curdle). Remove from heat and whisk in the vanilla, rum and butter. Serve sauce warm or cold. Makes 1⅔ cups.

CHOCOLATE SAUCE

1 cup sugar
3 tablespoons cornstarch
¼ teaspoon salt
1 cup cold water
1 ounce good quality unsweetened chocolate, cut in small pieces
2 teaspoons vanilla extract
2 tablespoons butter
⅓ cup whipping cream

In a medium saucepan combine sugar, cornstarch and salt. Stir in water and add the chocolate. Cook over medium heat, whisking constantly, until chocolate is melted and mixture is smooth and thick. Cool 5 minutes; stir in vanilla, butter and cream. Makes 2 cups.

RICH CHOCOLATE SAUCE

5 ounces semisweet chocolate, coarsely chopped
1 ounce unsweetened chocolate, coarsely chopped
¼ cup sugar
¼ cup hot strong coffee or espresso
2 tablespoons Grand Marnier*
2 tablespoons unsalted butter, room temperature

In a double boiler melt chocolates over hot, not boiling, water. Dissolve sugar in coffee and whisk into chocolate. Whisk in liqueur and butter until smooth. Makes about 1¼ cups.

*Rum, Amaretto or Frangelico may be substituted for the Grand Marnier.

SAUCE AUX FRAMBOISE

1 package (10 ounces) frozen raspberries (in sugar syrup), thawed
½ cup currant jelly
2 tablespoons cold water
1 tablespoon cornstarch

In a medium, heavy-bottomed saucepan bring raspberries and jelly to a boil. Combine cold water and cornstarch and whisk into raspberry mixture. Cook 1 minute, stirring constantly. Cool and strain through fine sieve. Makes 1½ cups.

GLAZES

APRICOT GLAZE:
1 jar (12 ounces) apricot jam
1 to 2 tablespoons brandy or fresh lemon juice

In a small saucepan melt jam over low heat. Remove from heat and strain into bowl; blend in brandy or juice. Cool to lukewarm before applying. Makes 1 cup.

RASPBERRY OR STRAWBERRY GLAZE:
1 package (10 ounces) frozen raspberries or strawberries (in sugar syrup)
½ cup currant jelly
1 tablespoon cornstarch
1 tablespoon cold water

In a small, heavy-bottomed saucepan bring berries and jelly to a boil. Combine cornstarch and water and add to berry mixture. Cook 1 minute, stirring constantly. Strain and cool to lukewarm. Makes 1⅓ cups.

ORANGE GLAZE:
1 12-ounce jar orange marmalade

In a small saucepan heat marmalade over low heat until melted. Strain and cool to lukewarm. Makes 1 cup.

NOTE Glazes are applied while slightly warm. They can be used to seal pastry, can serve as a simple icing and can be painted over the top of a tart to seal fruit from air and to give an attractive finish. Use a soft-bristle pastry brush to apply glaze.

TOASTING NUTS

Toast nuts on a baking sheet in a preheated 350°F. oven until lightly browned (Pine Nuts: 3 to 5 minutes; Almonds, Cashews, Hazelnuts, Pecans, Sesame Seeds and Walnuts: 5 to 7 minutes). Set timer for the shorter time; continue toasting, if necessary. Watch carefully that nuts don't overbrown or burn.

ROASTED FRESH CHILE OR BELL PEPPERS

Cut fresh peppers into quarters. Place on a broiler pan, skin side up, and broil until skin blisters and chars. Remove peppers from pan and place in a paper or plastic bag. Close bag and let peppers sit 15 to 20 minutes. Peel skin off of peppers.

NOTE Some people have skin that is very allergic to the oil released by peppers and should wear rubber gloves when working with any type of fresh pepper.

BREAD CRUMBS

For dry crumbs: Place slices of bread on a rack in a preheated 350°F. oven; turn oven off and allow bread to dry out. Break dried bread into small pieces and process in food processor or blender until crumbs form.

For fresh crumbs: Tear slices of fresh bread into pieces and process in a food processor or blender until crumbs form.

STERILIZING AND SEALING CANNING JARS
(For Jams, Jellies, Preserves, and Chutneys only)*

Place jars in a large saucepan, canning kettle, or roasting pan; cover jars with water. Bring water to a boil and boil for 20 minutes.

Place rubber seal lids in a saucepan and cover with boiling water off of heat source (boiling water softens rubber slightly and gives a better seal). When ready to fill jars, remove them from the boiling water and invert on a rack to briefly air dry; return to upright position. Fill with jam, jellies, preserves, or chutney, place rubber seal lid on top of jar and then screw lid on as tightly as possible with hand.

NOTE For best possible seal, jars should be very hot, and jam, preserves, chutney or relish at boiling temperature when placed in jar.

* For home canning fruits, vegetables, meat, fish or poultry, refer to a reliable canning procedure book.

SINGLE CRUST PASTRY

1⅓ cups sifted all-purpose flour
½ teaspoon salt
½ cup vegetable shortening
3 to 4 tablespoons chilled water

In a medium bowl combine flour and salt. With a pastry blender cut in half of the shortening until mixture is crumbly. Cut in remaining half of shortening (leave some of the pieces of shortening the size of lima beans). Add the water, 1 tablespoon at a time, stirring very lightly with a fork. After 3 tablespoons have been added, gather dough into a ball and press. If dough will not form ball and seems dry, add the remaining 1 tablespoon of water. Gather dough into a ball, press into a flat circle with smooth edges, wrap in plastic wrap and chill for 30 minutes.

On a lightly floured surface roll dough to a circle about 1½ inches larger than pie dish. Carefully pick dough up and gently ease into pie dish (do not stretch the dough).

With kitchen scissors trim dough to ¾ inch beyond edge of pie dish; fold under to make a double thickness of dough around the rim and flute with fingers, fork or pastry jagger.

For a single crust *baked without filling* prick bottom and sides thoroughly with a fork. Bake in a 425°F. oven for 10 to 12 minutes, or until golden brown.

For a single crust *baked with filling*, do not prick dough. Bake according to time and temperature recommended for filling used.

Makes one 9-inch pie shell.

DOUBLE CRUST PASTRY

2 cups sifted all-purpose flour
1 teaspoon salt
¾ cup vegetable shortening
4 to 6 tablespoons chilled water

In a large bowl combine flour and salt. With a pastry blender cut in half of the shortening until mixture is crumbly. Cut in remaining half of shortening (leave some of the pieces of shortening the size of lima beans). Add the water, 1 tablespoon at a time, stirring very lightly with a fork. After 4 tablespoons have been added, gather dough into a ball and press. If dough will not form ball and seems dry, add the remaining water, 1 tablespoon at a time. Gather dough into a ball, divide in two parts and press into

flat circles with smooth edges. Wrap in plastic wrap and chill for 30 minutes.

On a lightly floured surface roll bottom crust to a circle 1½ inches larger than pie dish. Ease dough into pie dish (do not stretch dough). Add filling. Moisten rim of bottom crust with water. Roll top crust to a circle 1½ inches larger than pie dish. Gently lift onto top of filled pie. With kitchen scissors trim dough to ¾ inch beyond edge of pie dish. Press the two crusts together to seal; flute with fingers, fork or pastry jagger. Prick or slit top crust to allow steam to escape. Bake according to time and temperature recommended in recipe. Makes one 9-inch double crust pie.

CRUMB PIE SHELL

1½ cups fine crumbs (chocolate wafers, vanilla wafers or graham crackers)
2 tablespoons sugar (optional)
5 tablespoons butter, melted

In a medium bowl combine crumbs and sugar, if used. Add melted butter and stir to combine. Press crumbs firmly and evenly into a 9-inch pie plate. Bake in a 350°F. oven 5 minutes; cool and fill. Makes one 9-inch crumb pie shell.

WHEAT GERM CRUMB CRUST

¾ cup graham cracker crumbs
¾ cup unsweetened flaked coconut
¼ cup wheat germ
6 tablespoons butter, melted

In a medium bowl combine crumbs, coconut and wheat germ. Add melted butter and stir to combine. Press mixture firmly into a 9-inch glass pie plate. Bake in a 375°F. oven 6 minutes. Makes one 9-inch pie shell.

PATE BRISEE

2 cups sifted all-purpose flour
1 teaspoon sugar
¾ teaspoon salt
¼ pound unsalted butter, well chilled and cut in 8 pieces
¼ cup vegetable shortening, well chilled and cut in small pieces
6 tablespoons chilled water
1 egg yolk

In a large bowl combine flour, sugar and salt. With a pastry blender cut butter and shortening into flour until crumbly; do not overwork. Whisk the water and egg yolk to blend. Add to dry ingredients and blend with a fork. Gather dough into a roughly shaped ball. On lightly floured board, knead dough into smooth ball. Wrap in plastic wrap and chill for about 30 minutes.

On a lightly floured surface roll out chilled dough ⅛ inch thick. Fit into tart pan with removable sides, pressing around bottom and sides. With kitchen scissors, trim dough to 1 inch beyond edge of tart pan. Fold overhang inside to form double thickness on sides and press firmly into place. Prick bottom and sides with fork. Line shell with cooking parchment; fill with dried beans or metal pie weights. Bake in a 400°F. oven 10 minutes. After 10 minutes, remove paper and beans; bake until light golden. Remove tart from oven and cool on rack. Makes one 10-inch tart shell.

PATE A CHOUX (CREAM PUFF PASTRY)

¼ pound butter
1 cup sifted all-purpose flour (sift flour over cup and level off)
¼ teaspoon salt
4 eggs, at room temperature

In a medium saucepan bring 1 cup water and butter to a rolling boil. Reduce heat to medium, add flour and salt all at once, stirring until dough forms a ball and looks like cornmeal mush. Remove from heat and cool for 2 minutes. Add eggs, one at a time, beating well after each addition. Using a large ice cream scoop or two large serving spoons, make 8 mounds of dough on a lightly greased cookie sheet.

Or, for appetizer puffs, use two teaspoons to form 24 mounds of dough on 2 cookie sheets.

Bake in a 400°F. oven 45 to 50 minutes for large puffs or 25 to 30 minutes for small puffs. Turn off oven and allow cream puffs to dry out in oven as it cools. Cut puffs in half and remove soft insides. Fill as desired. Makes 8 large puffs or 24 appetizer puffs.

POUND CAKE

¾ cup butter
½ teaspoon grated lemon peel
¾ cup sugar
3 eggs, at room temperature
1 teaspoon vanilla extract
1¼ cups sifted all-purpose flour
½ teaspoon baking powder
¼ teaspoon salt

Grease and flour the bottom of a 9-by 5-inch loaf pan. In a medium bowl cream together butter and lemon peel with an electric mixer. Gradually add sugar, beating until light and fluffy. Add eggs, one at a time, beating well after each addition; add vanilla. Sift together dry ingredients and add to creamed mixture; mix well. Turn batter into prepared pan; bake in a 350°F. oven 50 minutes, or until done. Cool in pan for 15 minutes, then remove and finish cooling on a rack. Makes 1 loaf.

FLUTED COOKIE CUPS

5½ tablespoons unsalted butter, softened
½ cup sugar
¼ teaspoon salt
2 teaspoons Grand Marnier
1 teaspoon finely grated orange peel
3 egg whites, at room temperature
½ cup plus 3 tablespoons all-purpose flour
¾ teaspoon cornstarch

Grease 2 baking sheets with vegetable shortening and flour the baking sheets; shake off any excess. Draw 2 circles (6 to 7 inches each) on each of the floured baking sheets.

In a medium bowl cream butter until fluffy with an electric mixer. Gradually beat in sugar; add salt, Grand Marnier and orange peel and mix thoroughly. Slowly beat in egg whites. Fold in flour and cornstarch until batter is smooth. Place 1 tablespoon of batter in center of each marked circle on baking sheet and spread with a spatula. The batter will be very thin. Bake 5 minutes, then start checking cookies (remove when just slightly browned). Remove each cookie with long metal spatula and invert onto a glass ramekin. Place another ramekin over the cookie and press into a flower shape. After 30 seconds remove ramekin and set cookie cups upside down on cooling rack. Makes 12 to 14 cups.

NOTE The cookie cups may be filled with ice cream, mousse, sorbet or fresh fruits with custard sauce.

BASIC PIZZA DOUGH

2 cups bread flour or unbleached all-purpose flour
¾ teaspoon salt
1 teaspoon dry yeast
⅔ cup to ⅔ cup plus 1 tablespoon warm water (105°F.)
1 tablespoon olive oil
Additional all-purpose flour

By hand: In large bowl combine flour and salt. Combine yeast and warm water and let stand 5 minutes. Stir in olive oil. Pour yeast mixture into dry ingredients and stir with a wooden spoon until ingredients are combined and form a rough ball of dough. Turn ball of dough out onto a floured surface and knead until smooth and elastic,

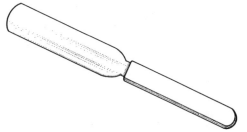

about 7 to 10 minutes. If dough is sticky, add additional flour to make a smooth and elastic dough.

With food processor: Place flour and salt in work bowl of processor and process using several on/off turns. Combine yeast and warm water and let stand 5 minutes; stir in olive oil. With machine on, add yeast mixture through feed tube. Continue processing until yeast dough is smooth, moist and well-mixed, about 7 seconds. Do not let dough form a ball. Turn dough out onto a floured surface and knead 3 minutes.

Form dough into a smooth, flat circle. Place dough on floured baking sheet. Cover with plastic wrap, allowing enough space between dough and wrap for expansion. Let rise in a warm, draft-free place for 1½ to 2 hours until dough doubles in volume.

Shape dough by using a rocking motion with fingertips to continually flatten and enlarge circle of dough. (Do not use a rolling pin. It will compress and toughen the dough.) To bake in a pizza pan: Complete shaping in pizza pan, forming a crust around the edge. To bake on a baking stone: Shape pizza dough on a baker's peel or rimless cookie sheet sprinkled with cornmeal. Form outer crust edge by pinching dough around edges. Bake according to recipe instructions. Makes one 14-inch pizza.

BASIC PASTA DOUGH

1¼ cups unbleached all-purpose
　　flour
½ cup semolina flour
1 teaspoon salt
2 eggs
2 tablespoons warm water
Additional unbleached all-purpose
　　flour

To mix in a food processor: Combine flour, semolina and salt in bowl of a food processor. Turn machine on and off twice to mix. Combine eggs and water. With machine on, add the egg-water mixture in a steady stream through the feed tube. The mixture should form a soft ball of dough. If dough is dry, add 1 teaspoon water; process to mix. If dough is sticky, add all-purpose flour, 1 teaspoon at a time, until the dough is smooth and elastic. To knead, process ball of dough about 40 seconds. Turn out on to lightly floured surface, cover with plastic wrap and let rest 20 to 30 minutes.

To mix by hand: In a large mixing bowl combine flour, semolina and salt. Whisk together eggs and water. Make a well in the dry ingredients and pour the liquid into the well. Combine with a wooden spoon or by hand. Gather pasta dough into a ball; place on floured surface, cover with plastic wrap and let rest 20 to 30 minutes.

To shape pasta dough with the hand-crank pasta machine: Divide dough into 3 equal parts. Work with one portion at a time. Cover other portions so they don't dry out. Feed dough through the smooth rollers of the machine set as far apart as possible. Fold dough into thirds, dust lightly with all-purpose flour if needed and feed through the machine again. Repeat 3 more times for a total of 5 feed-throughs.

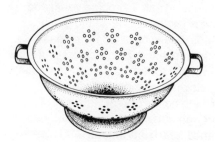

Set the rollers closer together (next setting) and feed dough through. Cut length of dough in half, if necessary, for easier handling. Set rollers to the next setting (closer together) and feed length of dough through the machine. (The number 5 setting is the top setting for most types of pasta.) Cut dough in half crosswise whenever needed, for easier handling. Feed the strips of dough through the blades of the cutting section. Place the cut pasta on floured waxed paper spread out on the counter or hang to dry on a pasta rack. Dry pasta for 30 minutes before cooking.

To cook fresh pasta: Bring 7 quarts water to a boil. Add 1 to 2 tablespoons salt and 1 tablespoon oil. Gently add the pasta. Stir with a spaghetti fork, separating the strands as they cook. Cook until al dente, about 2 to 3 minutes. Makes approximately 1 pound, or 4 servings.

NOTE If pasta dough seems sticky, dust lightly with flour between each setting before running through the machine.

RED BELL PEPPER PASTA

1 large sweet red bell pepper,
   roasted and skinned (page 126)
   or 1 canned roasted and skinned
   red pepper
1 teaspoon salt
1 teaspoon Hungarian paprika
2 eggs
½ cup semolina flour
1½ cups unbleached all-purpose
   flour

If using canned roasted pepper, remove any charred black skin that is
still present. In a food processor puree red bell pepper, salt, paprika
and eggs. (Or, puree in a blender or
with a food mill, add to liquid and
follow "To mix by hand" in Basic
Pasta Dough recipe.) Add semolina
and 1¼ cups unbleached all-purpose flour. Process until mixture
forms a ball of dough and pulls
away from the sides of the work
bowl. If dough is sticky, add as
much of the remaining ¼ cup all-
purpose flour as needed to form a
smooth and elastic ball of dough.
Process 40 seconds to knead. Turn
dough out onto lightly floured surface, cover with plastic wrap and let
rest 20 to 30 minutes. When pasta
is ready to shape, follow instructions for Basic Pasta Dough, page
130. Makes approximately 1 pound,
or 4 servings.

SPINACH PASTA

½ package (10 ounces) frozen leaf
   spinach, thawed
¾ teaspoon salt
2 eggs
½ cup semolina flour
1¼ cups unbleached all-purpose
   flour
Additional unbleached all-purpose
   flour

Cook the frozen spinach in ½ cup
water 3 to 4 minutes. Drain in colander until cool; squeeze all excess
water from spinach (spinach should
be as dry as possible). In a food
processor puree spinach, salt and
eggs. (Or, puree in a blender or with
a food mill, add to liquid and follow
"To mix by hand" in Basic Pasta
Dough recipe.) Add semolina flour
and unbleached all-purpose flour.
Process until mixture forms a ball
and pulls away from the sides of the
work bowl. If dough is sticky, add a
small amount of additional all-purpose flour as needed to form a
smooth and elastic ball of dough.
Process 40 seconds to knead. Turn
out onto a lightly floured surface,
cover with plastic wrap and let rest
20 to 30 minutes. When pasta is
ready to shape, follow instructions
for Basic Pasta Dough, page 130.
Makes approximately 1 pound, or 4
servings.

JALAPENO MOLE PASTA

2 eggs
Cocoa paste (1 tablespoon water
   mixed with 1 tablespoon plus 1
   teaspoon cocoa powder)
2 tablespoons finely minced fresh
   jalapeño pepper (2 small)
¾ teaspoon salt
½ cup semolina flour
1¼ cups unbleached all-purpose
   flour
Additional unbleached all-purpose
   flour (if needed)

In a food processor puree eggs, cocoa paste, jalapeño pepper and
salt. (Or, puree in a blender or with
a food mill, add to liquid and follow
"To mix by hand" in Basic Pasta
Dough recipe.) Add semolina flour
and unbleached all-purpose flour.
Process until mixture forms a ball of
dough and pulls away from the
sides of the work bowl. If dough is
sticky, add a small amount of additional all-purpose flour as needed
to form a smooth and elastic ball of
dough. Process 40 seconds to
knead. Turn onto lightly floured surface, cover with plastic wrap and let
rest 30 minutes. When pasta is
ready to shape, follow instructions
for Basic Pasta Dough, page 130.
Makes approximately 1 pound, or
about 4 servings.

menus

THE SUMMER BARBECUE

Green Bean and Walnut Salad, 63
Barbecued Flank Steak, 84
Fresh Corn Tortilla Casserole, 78
Peach Melba Mousse Pie, 110

INTERNATIONAL HOLIDAY BUFFET

Pesto Dried-Tomato Torta, 47
Crudités and Watercress Dip, 44
Marinated Shrimp and Pea Pods, 49
Pickled Mushrooms, 51
Tomato and Stilton Cheese Tart, 49
Oriental Chicken Wings, 53
Cocktail Puffs with Three Fillings, 54
Fresh Fruits with Amaretto Cream Cheese, 48
Persimmon Cake, 116

ITALIAN ANTIPASTI BUFFET

Crudités with Spinach-Basil Pesto Sauce, 47
Italian Carrot and Cauliflower Salad, 64
Herbed Chicken Breasts with Fresh Baby Artichokes, 90
Italian Quiche, 78
Fusilli with Tomato, Zucchini and Clam Sauce, 73
Pear, Gorgonzola and Walnut Filo Torte, 114

SUNDAY BRUNCH

Melon Soup with Strawberries, 61
Rolled Soufflé with Shrimp and Asparagus, 76
Spiced Chocolate Loaf, 117
Champagne

WINE COUNTRY DINNER I

Cream of Red Bell Pepper Soup, 56
Grapefruit, Papaya, Avocado and Watercress Salad, 67
Rack of Lamb with Balsamic Beurre Rouge, 85
Green Beans Sesame, 100
Pear Crisp with Calvados Ice Cream, 114

WINE COUNTRY DINNER II

Three Mushroom and Pine Nut Salad with Balsamic Vinaigrette, 62
Grilled Salmon with Red Bell Pepper-Basil Butter, 96
Wehahoma Rice Pilaf, 103
Fluted Cookie Cups, 129, with Tangerine Sorbet, 108, and Rich Chocolate Sauce, 125

UNDERTONES OF THE MIDDLE EAST

Wine Country Lemon Soup, 58
Avocado Shells Filled with Carrot and Orange Salad, 68
Spinach-Stuffed Leg of Lamb, 86
Wedding Pilaf, 104
Apricot Strudel, 114

FLAVORS OF MEXICO

Cold Cooked Shrimp and Crudités with Salsa Picante Dip, 45
Fresh Corn and Cilantro Soup, 57
Kiwi, Kumquat and Jícama Salad with Avocado-Lime Dressing, 67
Grilled Hibiscus Cornish Hens, 93
Orange-Caramel Flan, 110

CHINOIS

Chinois Scallop or Shrimp Salad, 83
Tangerine Sorbet, 108
Tea-Smoked Duck Chinois, 94
Hot and Sour Zucchini, 101
Almond Cake with Raspberry Sauce, 116

indexes

INDEX TO TOOLS

pastry scrapers, 24
pastry wheel, 21
pear corer, 14
peelers, 20, 22
pie weights, 21
pitters, 22
pizza cutter, 22
potato peeler, 22
poultry shears, 17
pounder, 17
pureer, tomato, 27

rolling pins, 22–23
rotary grater, 15
rubber scrapers, 24

scissors, 17
scoops, 23
scrapers, 24
shears, 17
shredders, 16
shrimp deveiner, 24
sieves, 13
sifters, 24
skimmers, 25
slicers, 12, 25
spatulas, 26
spatulas, wooden, 28
spice infuser, 26
spoons, slotted, 25
spoons, wooden, 28
spreaders, 26
strainers, 13
strawberry huller, 26
strippers, 20
stuffing needle, 21

tea ball infuser, 26
tea strainer, 13
tenderizer, 17
thermometers, 26–27
tomato corer, 14
tomato pureer, 27
tomato slicer, 25
tongs, 27
truffle slicer, 25
trussing needle, 21

vegetable peeler, 22

wheel, pastry, 21
whisks, 27–28
wooden spoons, 28

yeast thermometer, 27

zester, 20, 28
zucchini corer, 14

INDEX TO TECHNIQUES

appetizer shells, 30
apple slices for tarts and pastries, 38

balls, melon and food, 36
baskets, watermelon, citrus and
    tomato, 32
beaten egg whites, 41
beet shells, 30
bell pepper flowers, 34
boats, pineapple, 31
boning chicken, 40

cabbage shell, 31
carrot-flower coins, 34
cartwheels, citrus, 34
cherry tomato shells, 30
chicken, boning, 40
chicken, trussing, 39
chile pepper flowers, 34
chocolate curls, 38
chocolate leaves, 37
chopping, dicing and mincing, 40
citrus baskets, 32
citrus cartwheels, 34
citrus fruit, peeling and sectioning, 38
citrus peel roses, 34
citrus twists, 34
citrus zest, 35
crudités, 38

cucumber crescents, 37
cucumber shells, 30
cucumber slices, scored, 37

deveining and shelling shrimp, 39
dicing, 40
duck, trussing, 39

egg whites, whisked or beaten, 41

fans, radish and green onion, 36
filo leaves, 42
flowers, 34–35
flowers, pepper, 34
fluting mushrooms, 36
folding, 41
food balls, 36

green onion fans, 36

julienne cut, 40

kumquat flowers, 35

melon and food balls, 36
mincing, 40
mushrooms, fluting, 36
mushroom shells, 30

oysters, shucking, 39

pastry, rolling, 41
pear slices for tarts and pastries, 38
peeling and sectioning citrus fruit, 38
pepper flowers, 34
pineapple boats, 31
potato shells, 30

radish fans, 36
radish roses, 33
red cabbage shell, 31
rolling pastry, 41
roses, radish, tomato and citrus peel,
    33–34

scored cucumber slices, 37
sectioning citrus fruit, 38

INDEX TO RECIPES

ABOUT THE AUTHOR

Cooking has been Patricia Gentry's major interest since she was a child and was allowed to experiment in her parents' kitchen. She graduated from San Jose State University with a degree in home economics and presently works as a food consultant. She is also an instructor in home economics at Santa Monica College in Southern California and has taught classes in California Cuisine at UCLA Extension. While in college she was elected to Phi Upsilon Omicron, the national home economics honor society.